Reflections in Service

Memoirs of a Minister Turned Administrator
at a Retirement Home for the Elderly

1932-1997

A complimentary copy for you!
Merry Christmas

Paul G. Leaman
10/21/04

REFLECTIONS IN SERVICE
Memoirs of a Minister Turned Administrator
at a Retirement Home for the Elderly, 1932–1997
by Paul G. Leaman

Copyright © 2006
by Paul G. Leaman,
Leola, PA 17540, and Sarasota, FL 34232

All rights reserved.

The author was Administrator/CEO at Mennonite Home, Inc., 1520 Harrisburg Pike, Lancaster, Pa. 17601, from July 1, 1976, to August 31, 1997.

Scripture quotes marked KJV are from the King James Version of the Holy Bible. The others are from The Holy Bible, *New International Version* ®, copyright © 1973, 1978, 1984 by the International Bible Society; used by permission of Zondervan Publishing House; all rights reserved.

To order, please contact Paul G. Leaman:
14 Conestoga Manor Village, Leola, PA 17540 (summer)
or at 3907 Lemonwood Drive, Sarasota, FL 34232 (winter)
(peleaman58@juno.com)

Library of Congress Number: 2006907547
International Standard Book Number: 1-60126-001-6

Printed at
𝓜𝖺𝗌𝗍𝗁𝗈𝖿 𝒫𝗋𝖾𝗌𝗌
219 Mill Road
Morgantown, PA 19543-9516

Contents

Preface v

1. Early Life: Preadolescent Years 1
2. Elementary School Experiences 3
3. Who Am I? Teenage Years 8
4. Life's Meaning, Dating, Finding a Life Companion ... 12
5. Finding God's Plan for Service 17
6. Experiencing Different Cultures 21
7. Furthering My Formal Education 24
8. Following God's Further Leading 26
9. After Graduations, Moving On 28
10. When God Took Over! 32
11. Seeking God's Will in Decisions 35
12. A Definite Call to Administration 37
13. The Move to a New Job 45
14. Adjusting to a New Job 49
15. Rescued, Just in Time 52
16. Organizational Responsibility 55
17. Scared but Not Hurt 57
18. A New Building in the Making 60
19. Change, Change, and More Change 63
20. Stories of Residents 67
21. Yearning for Independent Living Services 89
22. Flying High and Having Fun! 94
23. Interesting Tidbits: Residents and Employees 98
24. Personal Encounters with Residents 106
25. Words of Appreciation Shared 114

The Author 123

Preface

The desire to write my memoirs and reflections for the years before and while I was serving at Mennonite Home has been growing on my mind and spirit since a formal retirement from the organization. While serving God in life and proclaiming the grace and salvation the Lord Jesus Christ, received by faith, I wish to share a story on the making of a life of service, and more particularly in administration at Mennonite Home.

Webster's Seventh New Collegiate Dictionary says: "A memoir is a narrative from personal experience; an account of something noteworthy; an autobiography." "Reflection is the production of an image by or as if by a mirror; something produced by reflecting; a thought, idea, or opinion formed or a remark made as a result of meditation."

This book presents some autobiographical material portraying experiences that shaped my mind and helped to make me who I became. It also shows how experiences and situations shaped my life in the making of an Administrator at Mennonite Home.

Before and since I wrote the hundred-year history of Mennonite Home, in a book entitled *On a Journey* (released May 6, 2003), employees (former and present) and some residents have encouraged me to tell my personal story. After much thought and prayer, I have decided to undertake the task. I had provided some of the following account as part of *On a Journey*, but we eliminated much of it in the final draft since it was more like personal memoirs than story of the organization.

Several acknowledgements are in order to recognize those individuals who so graciously assisted in formulating this manuscript. First, many thanks and appreciation to S. David Garber of

Scottdale, Pennsylvania, for the final editing of this manuscript. His patience, and enduring fortitude was very commendable as portions of this manuscript had to be re-written, some deleted, and re-arranged in format to bring it to excellent readable form. Thank you Dave, for a superb job in this final format, with deep appreciation for it's readability and clarity! God bless you!

Many thanks to my oldest sister Anna Leaman Geib, who graciously gave of her time to search for pictures of our "growing up" years, making them available from her personal scrapbook for copies to be included in this manuscript. Also, my faithful wife Erma Lois Groff Leaman, who helped "recall" various experiences and episodes of our 53 years together, and her diligent efforts in working full-time while I finished my formal education. She indeed is to be praised for diligently guiding and formulating principles of behavior, helping to shape our children's lives to serve the Lord Jesus Christ. God's blessings continue to be with you on a daily basis.

In addition, I would be remiss if the numerous employees stories and anecdotes were not included from former and present employees at Mennonite Home Communities. Among these are the following unique, and very qualified persons who were a joy to have on staff: Charlotte Yoder, RN, Director of Health Services; Linda Frankenfield, Director Human Resources; Karen Bauman, Secretarial Services; Henry Leaman, Director of Environmental Services; Gladys Bert, Director of Food Services; Pat Eckman, RN; Virgie Keener, LPN; Liz Funk, LPN; Sharon Honberger, CNA. May God bless each contributing person in their life in a unique way!

I intend these memoirs and reflections, telling of my experiences leading up to and including my twenty-one years of service, to honor God's blessings and grace and providential leading in my life and to encourage the ministry at Mennonite Home. Through this story, I challenge readers toward deeper commitments to God and his Son Jesus Christ, and to honor and glorify the Lord in their personal life. To this end, I humbly submit the following stories that come to mind as reflections on God's goodness, love, and grace!

Therefore, I humbly dedicate this book of memoirs to the one and only God of creation, who gave us minds to think, to remember and formulate thoughts to bless the lives of others. It is God our heavenly Father, with his Son Jesus Christ and the presence and power of the Holy Spirit, who sustains us in life and is worthy of our praise for his goodness to us. I also dedicate this book of memoirs to my deceased parents, family, teachers, and friends who played an important role in my growing-up years, and during the years of training, preparing me to serve God more effectively. I also dedicate these stories and memoirs to those who helped shape my life, allowing me to serve all the residents, employees, and trustees whom I worked for and with in these twenty-one years of service. May the Lord continue to bless the lives of each one as our great Creator God gives us life and breath to serve the kingdom of God.

Chapter 1

Early Life: Preadolescent Years

About the time when America was beginning to experience an economic upswing from the depths of the Great Depression, Father and Mother Leaman had the joy of Mother Leaman giving birth to her fifth child. It was about noon in a small clapboard siding house in the village of Witmer, Pennsylvania, on a hot sultry day, August 29, 1932. He was a small baby, a lively, kicking, and screaming little boy weighing almost seven pounds. They named him Paul. Incidentally, this name means small, and so he was, but nevertheless very much alive. Sanford D. and Mary N. (Groff) Leaman especially appreciated him, since the baby born a year earlier was stillborn. Three older siblings were living when Paul began his life's journey in the Leaman family. Then two sisters came along next, then three more brothers. However, the youngest only lived three days and was buried in the Mellinger Mennonite Church cemetery. I thus grew up with four living sisters and three brothers, making a living family of eight.

Paul soon learned what it was to take orders from those older than he: a big sister Anna; Chester next; then Miriam. The usual orders were: "Now it's time to go to bed. Did you go to the potty yet?" And later, as teeth developed in my mouth, "Did you brush your teeth?" Oh, how I hated to brush my teeth. It seemed as though the toothbrush would nearly choke me. I didn't like it at all! But as cavities set in, my dental trips for fillings were also filled with remorse for not taking care of my teeth as instructed by siblings and dentist. In fact, the dentist nearly scared me to death. To grind out the cavity in preparation for a filling, he insisted on injecting Novocain to deaden the nerve. I hated the sight of a needle coming toward me. He would always say, "It's far from the heart, far from the heart!" Then immediately he would pry my mouth open, stick the needle into my gum, and squeeze the plunger. Oh, how that did hurt! I would always "come to" a few minutes later, only to discover that he was holding my head down between my knees because I had fainted. A trip to the dentist is still not a picnic; I get uptight but have learned to take the experience a bit more in stride. However, I have made it a daily habit to brush my teeth, and if there is a cavity not too deep, I have let the dentist do the grinding without Novocain. How brave! My dear reader friend, how do you face the difficult experiences of life? Do you use a cop-out strategy? Or do you face the issue and ask God to help you cope with it? He will give the strength if you ask him!

Chapter 2

Elementary School Experiences

Within three to four years, Father and Mother Leaman had to move their growing family from the village of Witmer to the village of Smoketown, Pennsylvania, about two miles away. Father Leaman was a day laborer, working at a coal and lumber yard to support the growing family. When I was five years old, Mother Leaman sent me along with big brother Chester to a local grocery store to buy a loaf of bread. Chester had the dollar to pay for the bread, and I tagged along to get out of the way of the two older sisters, who were to help Mother make supper. Chester was somewhat bashful, and Mother had told me to keep quiet. So when we had walked to the grocery store, Chester gave the grocer the dollar for the loaf of bread. However, Chester did not say, "We want a loaf of bread." Since the grocer knew there were six siblings in the family, he gave us twelve loaves of bread. I had a huge armful of bread that was eight cents per loaf.

Mother Leaman was shocked to have so much bread. For several days we had peanut butter and jelly bread for snacks and at mealtimes. Did you ever have fresh peanut butter stick to the roof of your mouth? It's not funny, but my sisters thought so. Many times that happened to me, and I found it hard to talk with peanut butter stuck to the roof of the mouth. My sisters thought it was a good trick, helping to stop this chatterbox boy from trying to talk so much!

In 1938 I was turning six years of age just when a new school year was beginning. This was of real concern to my parents because I was small for my age and had developed a speech impediment: stuttering. Hence, my parents thought it best to keep me out of first grade until I would grow up some more. I likely inherited the speech impediment since I had an uncle, my mother's brother, whose speech impediment was so bad that it was difficult for him to talk and get his ideas across to anyone in a simple speech. As I remember him at family gatherings, he seemed to have an inferiority complex.

The decision to keep me home an extra year till I could grow up some more also gave me an increasing inferiority complex. It came from my speech impediment and not attending school with my own age group of cousins and friends. So I listened to the older group of siblings, who dictated the proper behavior for this puny little stuttering sibling. I resented this treatment and the authoritarian rule of the household telling me, "Stop talking until you can say it right." Well, what was right? I was doing my best with the impediment of speech, which was growing worse instead of better. I actually remember being afraid

The Leaman siblings, left to right: Anna, Chester (missing), Miriam, Paul (the author), Ruth, Irene, Sanford. Posing on the 1934 Ford sedan family car, well filled with parents and seven children.

of those older family members, especially of my father, who tried the best he knew to correct my stuttering.

After turning seven years of age in the fall of 1939, my parents finally enrolled me in the first grade at the Willow Street Consolidated Elementary School in Willow Street, Pennsylvania. We had moved again, to a rental house owned by a Harnish family, located along the Strasburg Pike and right next to the L. H. Brubaker Allis Chalmers implement dealer, in Lampeter Township. From here we children rode a bus to the Willow Street School. I felt inferior from being small for my age and one year behind the school class of my age group.

I was required to take a Saturday night bath with my brother siblings to save the hot water, which we heated on the cookstove and thriftily used for two boys at a time. Our house had no central heating system, so a small Perfection kerosene heater warmed the bathroom a bit. In a tousle with my brother, I was pushed back into the Perfection heater, and on my bare backside it branded me with the diamond-shaped trademark of the heater. I was branded so severely that even with salve and gauze over the wound, I could not sit comfortably. How was I to go to school, ride the bus, and sit all day in a school desk with such misery on my backside? Mother Leaman came to the rescue by making a puffed-up pillow for me to carry along to sit on in the bus and at my desk in school. That episode plunged me deeper into an inferiority complex for more weeks of the school year than I can remember.

Yet the first grade at Willow Street was also exciting. Have you heard of first-graders having a bout with puppy love? I was no exception. A cute little first-grade girl seemed to take a liking to me and I to her. We held hands and stumped around on the pavement at recess, trying to see who could stamp each other's foot the quickest. What a game that was! We received nothing more than a lot of exercise and some frustration from trying to stamp each other's feet. Perhaps that kind of game was the forerunner for the real dancing maneuvers of older persons.

By the time I was to enter second grade, Father and Mother Leaman had a deep concern about the public school system for educating their children. They helped to start a parents-supported parochial school near Smoketown, Locust Grove Mennonite School, and enrolled us siblings there. Parents took turns transporting their children by car to school each day.

By the time I was halfway through the fourth grade, Father and Mother Leaman bought a 120-acre farm near Conestoga Center, seven miles southwest of Lancaster. They wanted to give us growing siblings a better way of life. I was almost eleven years old that spring. Our life became busier: we had many chores to do before leaving for school and also right after we arrived home. There were chickens to feed, eggs to hunt, cows to milk, and then we had to do our school assignments before going to bed.

In those days there was no TV, so it was work, study, go to school—all on the same schedule day after day. Only occasionally did we play softball at recess while in school, for fun and exercise. Locust Grove did not participate in competitive sports with other schools.

Chester loading, with Paul driving the tractor: harvesting grass for hay. Sisters Ruth and Irene racking hay into rows on the lawn. Location: Strasburg Pike.

Locust Grove third- and fourth-grade students. Grace B. Lefever, teacher. Paul is first student on the right in row 2.

Entire student body at Locust Grove, grades 1–8. Grace Lefever taught grades 1–4; Walter Leatherman, grades 5–8.

Chapter 3

Who Am I? Teenage Years

Changing schools after three-quarters of the school year had elapsed was not easy for a young lad of nearly thirteen years, especially since I had a stuttering tongue and was one year behind others of my age group. However, at this young age I did not have time to ponder the implications of such a move for the future. Others often severely reprimanded me for not "talking right," but what could I do about the situation?

It was clear that my parents had purchased the 120-acre farm to give four growing boys and four growing girls plenty of work, to keep us out of mischief. To be sure, we had our sibling rivalry, skirmishes, and fear of punishment, when we heard the warning: "Just you wait till Papa gets home." The coal shovel waiting at the coal bucket was a quick and easy tool to use in bringing us into line. A parent would administer a few severe whacks across the backside for our misdemeanors and wayward conduct. The scripture says, "Train a child in the way he should go, and when he is old he will not turn from it" (Proverbs 22:6). Father and Mother Leaman, with no more than eight grades of schooling, did the best they knew in raising the family.

During these years of growing up, I developed in body and gained a greater understanding of the things of God and the story of Jesus Christ as Savior. I became aware of my shortcomings and need of a Savior through evangelistic sermons preached at church each fall. During my twelfth year, while attending such meetings, I felt the conviction from the Holy Spirit that I should accept Jesus into my heart and life. I responded when the invitation was given to do so while the congregation was singing an appropriate hymn, in meetings held at the Mellinger Church. I felt relief as the Lord lifted a burden from me. However, that experience still did not solve my stuttering problem; in fact, in some cases it seemed to be worse.

The decision to accept Jesus Christ as my Savior and Lord of one's life is the most important choice that each person must make for themselves if they want to live eternally with God through his Son Jesus Christ. If you are a reader who has never made that choice, you can accept Jesus Christ by faith, trust him for your life, and walk with him. There are three simple steps to meet the conditions as spelled out in God's Word: (1) Admit that you are a sinner (by human nature; Romans 3:10–12). (2) Confess your sinful condition without Jesus Christ, and ask God to forgive your sins (1 John 1:8–9). (3) In prayer, ask Jesus to come into your heart and life, and accept the salvation that God has provided for you in his great love, which is unconditional. Read the Gospel of John, chapters 1-3, and especially 3:1-21.

Later, with our move to the 120-acre farm, our parents transferred us children to a new school built by the local church folks: New Danville Mennonite School. Emily Kraybill, principal and teacher, administered the school and worked with several other part-time teachers instructing grades one through nine.

For entertainment, we siblings did some activities together. Since no TV was available then and our household did not even have a radio, we had to develop our own entertainment, be it games or just playing church, as we often did. The potential attendance was about six of the eight siblings, as I remember. One of the girls or a younger brother would be the song leader, and they drafted the stuttering brother to play the role of preacher. Since I had too much attention (the negative type) and the stuttering problem, just maybe being a preacher could have a positive effect. So they designated me to be the preacher in our sessions of playing church. I do not remember any texts for the sermons, or even responses to them, other than that the parishioners (siblings) were glad when I finally sat down. Could this have been a providential intuition of more to come?

The years of book learning at New Danville School were both challenging and embarrassing. Emily Kraybill, from Mt. Joy, was the principal and also taught several subjects to the lower grades. Grace Lehman, from Harrisonburg, Virginia, taught students in grades six through seven, and Roy Harnish taught grades eight and nine.

Ready for a snowball battle? After the big snow of 1947, families and neighbors shoveled the road open to haul the milk to a collection point. Roads were 14–16 inches deep, and no snowplows came near our farm.

I suffered through several embarrassing moments when I was required to recite or read an assignment in the front of the class, as did the other students. In one episode I distinctly remember, I had to be in front of the class to recite a portion of the lesson. My stuttering episode was so real and difficult that the teacher couldn't make much sense out of what I was trying to say. It caught the funny bone of this youthful teacher from Harrisonburg; she burst out laughing, yet turned her face the other way as best she could, trying to control herself. As it turned out, my classmates had to do the same. Why not? The teacher set the example! I was devastated, humiliated, and vowed in my mind to never read or speak in public again.

Furthermore, I began to dislike school more and more. What was I to say (or try to say) to my classmates when recess time came and we played outdoors? I was too embarrassed to join in the games or to be involved in more than a limited way. I certainly tried not to talk to anyone unless it was absolutely necessary.

In my ninth-grade experience, Roy Harnish as teacher ran things according to his strict disciplinary code, which reminded me of my father. Our parents did not believe it was necessary to go beyond the ninth grade since we could then obtain a work permit from the state, terminate our school learning, and stay home to work on the farm. Only after several years of being out of school did I develop a desire to earn at least a high school education, which could have happened earlier, since Lancaster Mennonite High School was then in operation. But no such luck! Perhaps more education at that point was only wishful thinking since I was a confirmed stutterer, and no solution seemed to be on the horizon.

I even found some advertisements in the *Successful Farming* magazine that came to our house, inviting stuttering handicapped persons to enroll in their school, somewhere in Illinois. One day I worked up enough nerve to ask my Dad about enrolling me in such a school. He said, "No, you can't go to such a place. We don't have the money, and it is too far from home. You belong here on the farm, working." I even had thoughts of running away from home but never did, knowing that the consequences if found and brought back would be severe. Reader, when you are tempted to run from your problems and/or situation in life, think again! Take your troubles to Jesus. "Cast all your anxiety on him because he cares for you" (1 Peter 5:7).

Chapter 4

Life's Meaning, Dating, Finding a Life Companion

The New Danville Mennonite Church had a membership of about 225. When we started attending there in the mid 1940s and early 1950s, it was a rural congregation, with mostly farmers and a few business people. There was an active youth group, which did projects sponsored by the parents or farmers in the congregation. The most exciting project was a Lord's Acre; each year the farmers took turns donating the use of one acre to plant tomatoes. Along with parents we young people would dedicate an evening a week to hoe the tomatoes, keeping the weeds out, and then picking the red ripe tomatoes. We hauled them to a collection station near Millersville, and trailer trucks took them to a processing plant in New Jersey. Other local farmers grew many acres of tomatoes for processing.

The Leaman family posing outside the big stone farmhouse. Left to right: In back, Father and Mother. Row 3, Chester, Anna, Miriam. Row 2, Paul, Ruth, Irene. In front, Daniel, Sanford.

At these young people's gatherings we learned how to mingle with others and chum with the boys and girls of the congregation. Boys even began talking to the lovely girls as we worked side by side in the Lord's Acre project.

The Leaman siblings, left to right: In back, Anna at 19, dating age; Chester, 17; Miriam, 15; Ruth, 11; Paul, 13. In front, Sanford, 7; Irene, 9; Daniel, 3.

My parents also raised as many as ten acres of tomatoes, to earn income and give us siblings some work. Once I became sixteen years of age, (late summer of 1948), I was able to acquire a driver's license and began taking my turn in driving my family's loads of tomatoes to the collecting station in Millersville. When I had the chance to have a load of tomatoes ready to leave early in the morning, about twice a week in the summer of 1949, I would try to time my trip to Millersville via the back country road past the farm where a lovely high school girl lived. The reason for the proper timing was that she had to walk to catch the school bus for a ride to her high school. If I timed the trip right, she was just beginning to walk to the school bus stop as I would go by their farm. As a seventeen-year-old chap, I eagerly looked forward to inviting her to ride with me in the old rattling truck instead of taking the one-mile walk. She always graciously accepted, so we had teenage chats for a ride that was much too short. Here she was, obtaining a high school education, which I could not get due to working at home on the farm. At times I certainly wished that I could have been going to high school and be in her class, but no such luck.

Anyway, the Lord's Acre project moved along smoothly. Eventually another lovely farm girl caught my eye at various times: Erma Lois Groff, who didn't go to high school either. At first she was somewhat shy, so to get her attention while picking tomatoes for the Lord's Acre project, I would sometimes throw a red ripe tomato her way. It really worked, because after I was eighteen years old, my family allowed me to start dating. I asked her out for a date and many more succeeding ones.

The buildings and livestock of the 120-acre family farm, with many cows to milk, eggs to hunt, and steers to feed.

Erma Lois was the oldest daughter of the deacon at our local church, New Danville Mennonite. I always liked the name Lois (her middle name), much better than the name Erma, but she wanted to be called Erma. Even to say "Erma Lois" would have been better than not to use Lois at all; but my suggestion for the change didn't carry enough weight, so we have stuck with the name Erma now for more than fifty years.

After two years of that type of activity, I popped the question of marriage. A year later we were married at the New Danville

Mennonite Church on Saturday morning September 5, 1953. During our dating years, however, we talked about future life activities and where we might want to serve the Lord Jesus. At times we prayed together and asked God's guidance for the future. The following Scripture was our guide and may be just what you need for your life! "Trust in the LORD with all your heart and lean not on your own understanding; in all your ways acknowledge him, and he will make your paths straight" (Proverbs 3:5–6).

During our courtship years, I told her how we siblings would play church and shared my feeling that someday a congregation might call me to be a real preacher, not just a fill-in for playing church. But what an assertive idea! With no high school education and a stammering tongue sometimes hard for others to understand, how could I be a preacher or a public speaker? Nevertheless, she must have had a lot of confidence in me because she kept allowing me to return for dates in those years.

About four months before our planned wedding date, church leaders asked us to attend a small mission church near Conowingo, Maryland. The New Danville congregation had started a church plant in that community. The Sunday school superintendent asked each of us to teach a Sunday school class for the smaller children. This went relatively well in spite of my speech handicap.

The New Danville District Mennonite churches—New Danville, Byerland, River Corner, and Rawlinsville—started this church plant around April 1950. They opened a Methodist building that had been closed for twenty-five years and supplied a preacher for the first three years. Each of these congregations had more than one minister, so a schedule was in place for a spare preacher to take a turn of driving to Maryland near the Conowingo Dam and bringing the Sunday message. This was the practice for about three and a half years until a regular minister could be ordained to serve this new and growing congregation. Leaders asked a core of church workers from established congregations to attend this embryonic church, to assist in the Sunday school teaching and outreach in the community.

After our wedding, we went on a two-week honeymoon trip to New England and Canada. By the end of September, we returned on Sundays to the mission, Oakwood Mennonite Church, and took up our class responsibilities. There the Sunday school superintendent told us about a prayer concern: the church leaders were making plans to ask the congregation to submit nominations for ordaining someone to be a minister in this new church. The choice was to happen by the end of October.

Chapter 5

Finding God's Plan for Service

Since I was twenty-one years of age and married only two months, Erma and I did not give much thought to the possibility that we might be among the nominated couples. Yet no one knew till the event arrived. The group of believers nominated four names. A huge shock came to Erma and me when the leaders announced my name as a possible candidate. Since I had a speech handicap, how could anyone dare to give my name? But someone or ones did, and that was that!

The bishop announced a meeting date when all four men with their respective wives would meet with the district's church leaders for a questioning period. Leaders would examine the nominees regarding their walk with the Lord Jesus and ask if they had a call to the ministry! In those days, from little up we were taught to respect the church leaders, never to question their wisdom or decisions, and to participate in whatever the church asked us to do. This experience was no exception. However, I thought, *But why me?*

Just two weeks later, after thorough examinations and filling out questionnaires, all four men with their companions agreed to participate in the process of finding God's choice in this matter. The leaders scheduled the ordination service for Sunday afternoon, November 21, 1953. In those days, when the congregation needed only one man to become the new minister but members nominated several, the leaders used the lot to determine God's choice in the matter.

For casting the lot, the church used four hardcover Bibles, in keeping with the number of men in the ordination class. The bishop in charge of the service asked two ordained men from the gathering to take these four Bibles to a Sunday school room. One of them placed a slip inside the front cover of one Bible, bearing a verse: "The lot is cast into the lap, but its every decision is from the LORD" (Proverbs 16:33). Then they shuffled the Bibles so that no one knew where the slip was. They carried the Bibles to the bishop in charge, who mixed them again as he placed them on the pulpit, standing in a straight row.

The bishop led the congregation in an extended prayer to God for the Holy Spirit to lead each man in choosing a Bible. Then he said, "Now, brethren, take courage and choose a Bible as long as there is a choice, starting with the oldest man." About two hundred people packed the small church building for this far-reaching and momentous event. As the congregation waited, the oldest candidate chose a Bible, and so did each succeeding man till only the last Bible remained. As the youngest man, I took the last Bible.

The bishop, beginning with the oldest, opened each Bible till he found the slip of paper with the Bible verse on it. The slip was in my Bible. It was a very emotional experience; the atmosphere was highly charged with suspense. I immediately had a shock of disbelief but could not evade the call of God. My emotions broke loose. I cried quite openly, and many in the congregation were doing the same, including my beautiful young bride of two months. The bishop immediately ordained me to be pastor of that congregation.

Soon thereafter, the district's church leaders called a meeting with my wife and me and other ministers to lay further plans for this newly ordained young man and his wife, to support him in the work of ministering to the congregation. What? A stuttering young man called to preach soon? During this whole process of discernment, not one of the church leaders questioned my qualifications to preach or lead a growing congregation of people. Here we were, married two and a half months, with no formal training. I was a stuttering young man, yet called by God through the lot (and through earlier inklings along the way that God might call me sometime)

Furthermore, at the close of the planning session, the bishop looked at me and said that in two weeks it would be my turn to preach my first sermon to this congregation. Wow! At home I fell to my knees, pouring out my heart to God and asking for direction. I wouldn't dare to buck the church leaders and say "No way!" That was unheard of! So I went to God in prayer, asking him to heal my stuttering tongue if it is his will to do so. Well, why wouldn't it be his will? Would he want a young man to be continually embarrassed up front?

As I (and others, I am sure) prayed for my healing, I felt the Lord's presence, and his Holy Spirit flooded my soul and body in the healing he gave me that day. I was healed! Praise God! That day as I was on my knees before God, the Lord purged my speech of stuttering, and I have had complete healing from that day on. Praise God! Now, if you as a reader have difficulties in life, go to God in prayer. If you know him as Savior and Lord, he loves you and cares for you immensely. If you do not know Jesus Christ, first give your heart and life to him; then he will do for you what is his plan for your life! Praise God!

Now that God took care of my physical problem, would he also care for my spiritual challenge? Would he tell me how to prepare messages to share to a people who have problems and challenges in life just like my own?

Sure enough, a fellow minister gave me a really nice gift; *The New Chain-Reference Bible*, edited by Frank Charles Thompson (King James Version, 1929). This gift was a valuable tool for Bible study since I did not have the opportunity to take formal Bible training at any school of higher learning. In fact, I did not even have a high school diploma, so how could I get into a college program if I wanted to? Furthermore, preachers were not salaried in those days, as they are now, and I had a lovely wife to support, too.

A good brother in the home church at New Danville helped me find a daily job at a John Deere Implement Shop about fifteen miles from the church I was to pastor. At that time we lived about three miles from the church. I needed to work an eight to nine hour day at $1.25 per hour, thus supporting my stay-at-home wife, who became a mother to our first son by May 4, 1955. We believed it was a God-given right, privilege, and fulfillment to have a family, so for the next ten years we were blessed with a family of three boys, then a daughter, and the final child (a son), completing a family of five children.

It was a challenge for us to raise five children under the scrutiny of the public watching how we do it and expecting the best conduct from everyone of this group of imperfect people. Even preacher's kids (PKs) needed the love, grace, forgiveness, and mercy of God for every situation that occurred in life. God is good, and we trusted in him, believed in him, and taught the truths of God's Word to the children. That is the best heritage parents can give.

The longer we served at this growing congregation of believers, the more I desired to further my education, desiring to be more effective for God's work. But how could a young growing family pull up stakes and move? How could I go back to school and study with no income for a growing family? I dreamed of having a church to pastor where I would be salaried, but there were not many available in those days, and certainly not for someone without an education and training.

Chapter 6

Experiencing Different Cultures

However, after serving this congregation for thirteen years, I felt a need for a change, talked to the bishop in charge and he thought there would be another brother who could serve in the capacity of preacher. We had also received a call through mission personnel in Atmore, Alabama, to move south and take over the pastorate of a mission church (Poarch Community Church). A Creek Indian tribe there supplied some believers, and the mission hoped that many more of them would become believers.

The mission promised me up to half-time support to serve this congregation. We sought the Lord's leading, sold some things in Pennsylvania, and moved about thirteen hundred miles, with a family of five children, to a poor area of the country, to serve a people who needed to learn more of the love of Jesus.

The Indian culture was so much different from ours. We had a lot to learn, but yet they had the same spiritual

The Leaman family of (from left) Pastor Paul (author), Erma Lois (wife), Jay, Carl, Stephen, Naomi, and Paul Jr., at author's sister's farm for family time just before moving south to Atmore, Alabama, in August 1966.

needs in their souls and life as all other people. They even had different ways of expressing their need to us when they needed some help. One day while visiting a three-hundred-pound Indian lady in her home, she said she needed a ride to town about ten miles away, to do some shopping. She did not drive and neither did her husband, so she asked me if I would "carry" her to town. At first thought I almost gasped, but then I realized that was their way of asking for a ride in my car. I was not muscular enough to "carry" her to town.

A different culture indeed it was, and we learned many other nuances of that culture that are not part of this story. Essentially, we needed to learn about five cultural streams that met us in the southland: the Creek Indian tribe, the white Americans (southern style), the deep south African Americans, the intermarriage of whites and African Americans, and in a few situations the Creek Indians intermarrying southern whites and African Americans. What a mix! God really gave us a challenge to minister to these varied and different cultures. This really opened up a new wound in my spirit. I still had that underlying desire to have more formal education, to give me greater insight into the challenges facing us as a family as we served in church and community.

Incidentally, the current President/CEO at Mennonite Home Communities is J. Nelson Kling. When I first met him, he was a sixteen-year-old youth living close to the Poarch Community Church, where we were serving. His parents had moved south from Pennsylvania in 1948, to establish a mission church in the area. Nelson was born in Atmore, Alabama, in June of 1950. He assisted in Saturday-evening volleyball games with our church community youth. I was favorably impressed with his candid personality, his positive attitude, and his help in winning some of the volleyball games. Just two years later, we studied together when I began taking courses at the Bay Minette Junior College, and he was there too, fresh out of high school.

We as a family moved to Harrisonburg, Virginia, in the spring of 1970, and later (in 1976) to Lancaster, Pennsylvania, so I had lost track of Nelson until the fall of 1988. Then we both found ourselves becoming reacquainted by singing together in the Men's Chorus named the Singing Men of Praise. On a chorus tour into Canada, we sang at several churches, and en route I had an opportunity to chat with Nelson about my work at Mennonite Home (see chapters 12 and following). I was in need of a Housekeeping Manager, which did not interest him. Later, when I approached him about becoming my assistant in developing the projected Independent Living section of the campus, I caught his interest. To read the story of how that part of the campus came into being, get a copy of *On a Journey*, authored by Paul G. Leaman, the story of the hundred-year history of Mennonite Home Communities. Copies are available at the Mennonite Home main office and are well worth your time in reading.

Pastor Paul G. Leaman, as shown in the Atmore Advance newspaper, introducing Paul as the new pastor.

Poach Mennonite Gospel Mission. Attendance grew from 25 to 65 persons in three years.

Chapter 7

Furthering My Formal Education

Before moving south, I did go to Millersville University (near Lancaster) and took the courses needed to earn my Commonwealth Secondary School Diploma in the spring of 1966. This qualified me to enter college sometime, somewhere. After one year of living in Atmore, Alabama, in the Deep South, I enrolled in the Bay Minette Junior College, starting on a course that would eventually take me through the freshman and sophomore years there.

After serving the Creek Indians a total of four years, an unfortunate situation that developed in the community led us to believe it was not wise to raise our family in that environment. Also, I was still nursing a desire to become a graduate of Eastern Mennonite College (EMC) someday. We talked it over with Home Missions personnel, who released us from our assignment at the Poarch Community Church.

I was not adequately prepared for the frustrations and stress that came from ministry in the varied cultures of the Deep South. Perhaps the best term to use is that I was "burned out." There was a real need for a change. So, we packed up again and moved to Harrisonburg, Virginia, by the end of May, 1970.

I was able to transfer most of my junior college credits to a four-year college, Eastern Mennonite University (EMC at that time). To finish, I went to summer school two summers straight plus two years of regular semesters, graduating May of 1972 with a B.A. degree in Bible and Psychology. Then I continued on into a three-year master's program in the seminary on the same campus. I earned a master of divinity (M.Div.) degree, graduating in May 1976, and served as president of the senior class. I thank the Lord many times and express great appreciation for the opportunity he gave me to acquire additional tools, usable in ministry where the Lord would lead us.

Chapter 8

Following God's Further Leading

The change by moving to Harrisonburg, Virginia, was a very good experience for us as a family. We enrolled our teenage children in Eastern Mennonite High School (EMHS). The first two years 1970–1972, I was busy taking full-time studies, meeting people, making new friendships, and being available for service in the ministry if God should so lead. In fact, there were plenty of opportunities for preaching assignments, a three-month interim in a mission church near Harrisonburg, and joining a men's chorus.

I also had carpenter and construction skills from early in our married life. In fact, we (I and several employees) had engaged in contracting, building new kitchen cabinets and even one new house a year for about seven years. However, after we moved to Harrisonburg, I had no time to use my construction skills while going to EMC as a full-time student. However, our four growing sons needed summer work. So with my construction skills, one employee with some carpenter skills (also a part-time student at EMC), and our boys willing to learn, we built a new house for customers each summer. My management and administrative skills seemed to come alive in this new endeavor by our family. I would get the carpenter crew going on the job each morning, check on their progress at noontime, and review their progress each evening. The customer paid to have the house built, our sons learned what it was to earn money, and I had fun with my diversion from studies for managing the construction work.

Erma, my wife, took a job in dietary services at the Virginia Mennonite Home after our youngest was in elementary school.

She really earned the PHT degree (Put Husband Through), to subsidize our income to stay afloat financially. She worked in this job for all of the six years we lived in Harrisonburg. Our time there was from June 1, 1970, and then moving back to Lancaster, Pennsylvania, by June 1, 1976. During these six years in the Shenandoah Valley of Virginia, our two youngest children were in elementary schools, while the three oldest boys were somewhere in college. Jay, the oldest, attended EMC, earned a bachelor of science (B.S.) degree in math and science, and then began teaching in a Shenandoah Valley school. Our second son, Carl, went to Hesston College in Hesston, Kansas, earning a two-year degree in business. Stephen, our third son, attended EMC, earning a B.S. in science and biology, eventually acquiring a teaching position in Broadway High School.

During our first two years at Harrisonburg, our family of seven lived in the mobile home park on the campus of EMC. Can you imagine a family of three growing teenage sons in the early stages of social friendships, both with their school and church associates, and two others (a preteen daughter and son), all living together in a mobile home? It was a two-bedroom unit, plus a large bedroom built on the side of the unit, where our four boys slept in two beds. We had a closeness of family when we all appeared in the kitchen for breakfast, and then again for a meal near the end of the day. Our contacts throughout the day were scarce: Erma worked full-time in the kitchen at the Virginia Mennonite Home, Paul was in classes all day or in the library studying to keep up good grades, and all the children were off to high school and elementary school. So we met twice a day (morning and evening), with Saturday and Sunday each week being a reunion time, to learn what we were doing and who we were. It was almost like camping out every day, and it made a good experience for the whole tribe.

The house building continued, with customers paying to have a house built during the summer months. Thus we were able to earn tuition money and have a stream of income, to keep bills paid and food on the table. It was a great life.

Chapter 9

After Graduations, Moving On

Rather late one evening, I was helping the construction crew to get a house finished and was brush-painting the varnish on the hardwood floor in a new house. The local Eastern Mennonite High School principal (Sam Weaver) stopped by to say hello and something more. We had known each other for many years, and even as school chums in elementary school many years before. He wanted to know if I would be interested in joining his staff at the high school, to be its first development director.

The board had approved the building of a new gymnasium for the high school students. It became a major project to raise thousands of dollars to build this new building. As development director, the job offer was to help raise the money from donors and patrons of the school, recruit students for each coming school year, and teach a Bible course in the classroom on Tuesday and Thursday each week. I was flabbergasted with the offer. Since I had never done anything quite like it before, I wasn't sure how to answer his request.

My first interest and impression was to seek God's direction in this matter and share the idea with my wife and family. This was in the late summer of 1972. I had just graduated from EMC that past May and was looking forward to attending Eastern Mennonite Seminary in the fall, which had accepted me as a full-time student. It was on the same campus, close to the college. The principal assured me that courses were available in the evenings and early mornings at the Seminary. Hence, I could still work in this new proposed job the rest of the day and on Saturdays, visit

Virginia Conference churches on weekends, and be paid for a full-time job.

After much prayer for guidance from God, his Holy Spirit, and counsel with and from the family, I accepted the proposed new job as development director. My new boss was an energetic man, and he knew the Virginia Conference and business community well. He would send me to some well-informed friends of the high school, asking me to make a visit and bring back some sizable checks for this new gymnasium project. Since I had never done anything quite like this before, I wondered many times how this would fit into a full-time pastorate in some church after I graduated from seminary. As it turned out, after several months that first school year (in the fall of 1972), I really began to have some marginal success at fund-raising, meeting many new friends, and learning how to be involved in development work.

By this time, after living in a house trailer for two years, we as a family were becoming restless in the confined quarters of our temporary housing. So, with funds from the sale of our house in Alabama, we bought a vacant lot in a housing development about a mile from the EMC campus. After official approvals, we found the right floor plan for a new house and proceeded to build. This was exciting, but I had only marginal time to work on the project. Even though fairly young, sometimes we were exhausted. We occasionally found some time to rest and sleep as we plodded on to the completion of the house. It surely was good to have three teenage sons to assist. However, due to our schedule of work, study, and family togetherness, our children never had time to become deeply involved in sports. We as parents felt that what we were doing provided enough exercise to keep their bodies healthy and growing.

At the same time, I was studying late most every night in the college library, trying to stay up with my daytime classes at the seminary. It soon became clear that I could not handle a full-time load of studies on marginal time. So I changed my class schedule to be three-fourths time, completing a three-year M.Div.

degree over four years. This was satisfactory to the dean at the seminary, and it worked out well for my schedule. However, that would have me graduating from seminary by the spring of 1976 rather than 1975.

Several pastors of Virginia Conference churches let me speak on behalf of the high school about the need for increased giving and Christian stewardship. I was beginning to like the job for the school, and yet a strong underlying conviction for serving as an ordained minister was in my thinking. After what God had saved me from, and the healing he gave me with the ability to speak rather fluently, I could not easily shake off the call to ministry. In sharing with my boss about my struggling thoughts, he assured me that what I was doing was indeed a vital part of the ministry of the church, and that I should pray about it and continue in this important work. Actually, I began to like being a development director, meeting many new people, and getting a livable wage while doing it.

However, I also kept in touch with the bulletin board postings of the need for pastors among congregations of the broader church. I replied to several churches where church boards were looking for trained pastors. Sometime during my second or third year of seminary training, my wife and I interviewed with representatives of a Mennonite Church in northwestern Pennsylvania. It was snow country, to say the least. The interview went well, but neither the church board nor we as a pastor couple made any commitments. I felt led not to rush into any long-term commitment with a church group prematurely, and I did want to finish my seminary degree. So Erma and I mutually agreed to allow more time to process any invitations to a specific congregation.

My development director job for Eastern Mennonite High School, even went far beyond the Virginia Conference supporting churches. My job description required a trip to Sarasota, Florida, every winter during Christmas break at the seminary, when classes were suspended till after New Year. The trip to Sarasota was to recruit students for the junior and senior years from

Mennonite Churches. There was a Sarasota Christian School serving that area, but it did not yet have a high school curriculum. Any students recruited from Sarasota would live in the dormitory at EMC for their junior and senior years. It was a good way to have students mingle with others from Virginia, Ohio, Michigan, and New York, since those areas of the Mennonite Church did not yet have a Mennonite high school in their areas or (in Ohio) had a tradition of sending students to Harrisonburg.

In addition to the Sarasota trip at Christmastime, I was also responsible to visit Ohio, Michigan, New York, and western Pennsylvania for students and for funds to support the EMHS budget. During each spring break, I made the Pennsylvania, Ohio, Michigan, and New York ten-day trip. The trip of 1973 to these areas was my first. The principal of EMHS gave me a geographical outline of places to visit and identified families with high-schoolers and businessmen who were supporters of the school.

Chapter 10

When God Took Over!

On this particular trip of 1973, I chose to go via Chambersburg, Pennsylvania, to visit the first area on the route. I personally knew several businessmen in that area, so the initiation of this new job would be easier, according to my way of thinking. It was a cold spring, warming up some days, with just the right kind of nasty weather to torment a busy student and development director with a bad head cold and congestive sinuses. I stopped in Chambersburg to buy some cold relief medications and to get directions to my first stop for the school.

After making my purchases, I asked how to find my client's place of business. The cashier in the store said, "Go back the way you came and turn left after six blocks, go out of town to . . ." Chambersburg streets were strange to me, but I did as told, and went back the way I had come, not realizing until two blocks down the street that I was driving the wrong way on a one-way street. All of a sudden another vehicle was coming right for me on a slight curve in the street, so I immediately hit the breaks hard, making black marks on the roadway, turned to my right, and skidded to a stop up against the curb, just missing a fire hydrant.

I was stopped but still in the line of traffic for the other vehicle. That driver had no choice but to hit my vehicle straight on at about thirty-five miles per hour. He had swerved some, but the impact drove the left front of the 1972 Dodge school car I was driving the whole way back to the firewall.

The steering wheel impacted my body with significant pressure on my stomach and abdomen. The split seconds of this all happening sent quick flashes of thoughts through my mind. I actually thought this could be my last day on earth. Even though I was wearing a seat belt, violent impact threw me forward while the car wreckage came toward me, causing my head to strike the windshield. I suffered a hairline cut on my forehead and a bruised head, with not much room left for my legs on the car's floor. The other driver was alone and did a remarkable job of slowing as much as he could in the seconds when this all happened. Emergency workers took him to the hospital for an exam, which only found his front teeth knocked loose from impacting the steering wheel.

Just moments before all this occurred, God spoke through his Spirit to the English teacher at EMHS while she was interviewing a student in her office. This English teacher was a spiritual-minded person and often shared with me about her walk with God, since her office was right next to mine in the school building. The Holy Spirit prompted her to "dismiss the student and pray for Paul right now because he is in deep trouble." This was at 11:03 a.m., and this accident occurred at 11:05 a.m. As I was being involved in this tragic accident, I felt the warmth of God's presence, with his angels surrounding me in that car as the inevitable happened.

Do I believe in miracles and the power of prayer? Indeed I do! As saying goes, "God is not through with me yet!" I believe that. Do you as you read this? Have you experienced God's presence so real that he floods your soul and body with protection when needed? Praise his wonderful name! Life is uncertain, so I invite you, dear reader, if you have not accepted Jesus as your Savior and Lord, to do it now, since life is so uncertain at its best.

This experience taught me to be more careful in my driving, to recognize God's presence and leading in all of life's decisions, and to thank him for sparing my life. After the police officer cited me for reckless driving and the tow trucks pulled the cars off the street, the officer took me to a car rental business and to make several phone calls. I called my wife to report that I was OK! I also called my office and talked to my boss. He suggested I get a motel, take several sleeping pills, and sleep. So I did. The next morning I was so stiff that I could hardly move.

After a breakfast, I proceeded on my journey with the rental car to complete my ten days of contacts. My trip and contacts through Scottdale, Pennsylvania; Mt. Gilead, Ohio; and Pigeon, Michigan, were profitable for the school, and several students decided to enroll for their high school years. However, as I traveled eastward, I learned by radio that upstate New York had four feet of snow, so I conveniently turned south, intercepted I-81, and reached Harrisonburg safe and sound.

The next morning, I met the praying English teacher, who asked me to come into her office. I did, and she told me in fine detail how the Holy Spirit spoke to her to dismiss the student and pray for Paul because he is in deep trouble. We both prayed again, thanking God for his blessings of life, direction in life's experiences, and for his safety on our lives and on the highway. Actually, the whole faculty heard how God worked through his obedient children, giving us more reasons to praise him!

Chapter 11

Seeking God's Will in Decisions

There were numerous appreciative comments from our friends in the community and church for my work with EMHS as development director. I actually learned to like my work and value the many friends and families in the Harrisonburg and other areas that I had the privilege to meet. God is good! He blesses us in such remarkable ways. How dare we question his leading? The studies in seminary were going well. I was raising funds for the high school budget and teaching Bible in the classroom two sessions per week. Future thoughts and plans were for me to graduate by the spring of 1976. Then what?

Our children were doing well in school and college. Erma was doing what she liked, working with others in the kitchen and cooking meals at Virginia Mennonite Home, which provided nice facilities for those living there in retirement. However, after two years of living in a mobile home, we needed more room. The trailer park was right across the street from the high school building and convenient for our busy schedules.

After much thought and prayer, we decided to use the funds from the sale of our house in Alabama and build one big enough for our family of teenagers. We found a nice building lot about one mile from campus, on the east side of the street, thus giving us a beautiful view of Massanutten Peak in the Blue Ridge Mountains. We started building this house in the spring of 1972 and launched a heavy work schedule, to have much of it built before school started in the fall (see chapter 9). Subcontractors with expertise or specialized tools did some of the work. We moved into the house around Christmas of 1972. To accommodate our family of four sons and one daughter, the house had a full basement and four bedrooms.

I received many confirmations by school faculty, church friends, and family support for my work with the high school. I was having fun, gaining an education from school patrons, students, businessmen, and others, and even getting paid to do it. As I worked with students already at EMHS and recruited new ones, all the while I was getting older. It occurred to me that I may not want to do this job indefinitely. What if the youths came to regard me as being "over the hill"? Then what would I do? But until God would lead me otherwise, I was content to continue on with what I was doing.

The principal of the high school was a good mentor for me to learn administration work. One of his favorite statements in dealing with people, and especially youthful students, was using "the element of surprise." So, if it was fund-raising (which he was good at), or giving me and the faculty statements to challenge us in our work, he was overjoyed to always inject some surprise. He was a good school administrator and wanted me to learn to be the same.

Nevertheless, the biggest "element of surprise" came to us as a family in the winter of 1973. While visiting family in the Lancaster area, a board member of Mennonite Home asked me to consider becoming the Administrator of that retirement home in Lancaster, Pennsylvania. I quickly replied to the inquirer that I had no interest in moving now, nor was I interested in working with those "old people."

When I was a teenager, we young people would go to Mennonite Home once or twice a month to "sing" for the elderly. As I remembered that place in the mid to later 1940s, it was a place where "old people sat around, with not much to do, and looked quite worn out." The buildings looked the same, definitely outdated and in much need of remodeling and modernizing. But we as young people had the excitement of our social life in going to sing for these "old people." It was a good activity. So with those reflections lingering in my mind, my wife and I dismissed the inquiry and let it drop.

Chapter 12

A Definite Call to Administration

But behold, the Mennonite Home Board of Trustees did not give up that easily! While living in Harrisonburg and in studies up to my ears, we eagerly looked at all mail, especially if it bore a Lancaster postmark.

February 19, 1974, was bitterly cold and blustery in the Shenandoah Valley of Virginia. I had just come home between classes at Eastern Mennonite Seminary. As I picked up the mail and felt the biting wind and chilled fingers, more snow definitely seemed to be in the air. I turned into the house, stomped some snow off my shoes, and glanced at the mail that had come. Among the bills and letters was one bearing a postmark from Lancaster, Pennsylvania, with a return address of Mennonite Home. *"What would that place want with me?"* I thought as I ripped open the envelope and quickly scanned the letter. I soon realized that the Board had authorized the chair of the Human Relations Committee to write the letter.

"Honey, guess what I got in the mail today?" I called to my wife.

"Oh, I don't know," she replied. "Probably a letter from a church wanting us to come to be their pastor couple."

"No, it's a letter from the chair of the Human Relations Committee of the Board at that Old People's Home at Oreville, near Lancaster—you remember, where we used to go to sing when we were teenagers?"

"Oh yes, I remember," she replied. "But what do they want you to do at that old outdated place?"

"They are asking if I would consider coming to be their new Administrator by the spring of 1975 or as soon as possible!"

Erma replied, "Oh no! I thought we were going to take a church somewhere. What did you tell them?"

"Why, nothing yet. I just received the letter in the mail today!"

"Do you want to go? What would you have to do?" Erma asked.

"Wow," I replied, "just a minute: that's too many questions at once. We need to find out more information."

"What do you want to do? Do you really want to go?" she asked.

I replied, "I really don't know enough about the job offer and what the job requires to give any intelligent answers at this point. They only want to know now if I am interested, and how soon we could move, if I am sincerely interested. Here is the letter for you to read."

After Erma read the letter and I reread it several times, it was time for me to be back in class. At this point in time, we agreed that we would need to make a decision, but only after much soul-searching, prayer, and discussion with our children and others in our church family. During the next several classes, I did have mingled thoughts, trying to concentrate on the studies at hand while my mind kept wandering around the country, and wondering what all could be involved with this job offer in Lancaster. We did acknowledge receiving the letter from the Mennonite Home Human Relations Committee by writing a short response, letting them know that we need some time to sort out all the implications of such a move.

What was that the seminary professor just asked? Did I miss something? The student next to me said, "He is asking what a 'metaphor' is. Do you know?"

"Isn't it a literary device or figure of speech in which the word used is to mean a certain object or thought?"

In the back of the room was a young student fresh off the farm and studying to become a pastor. He replied to his colleague, "That is what we had a 'meadow for' at home, to let our cows graze the grass." His two buddies on each side of him really cracked up laughing. Fortunately, the professor didn't catch the joke, so class proceeded as usual. Those three students told the rest of us after class in study hall, and did we ever have a renewed time of laughter. As far as I know, the conservative no-nonsense professor never did hear that joke.

That same evening, after we all were home again from our studies and Erma from her dietary job, we agreed to set aside a time for a family night of discussion on the proposed Lancaster option. The date was set, and we expected to have an exciting time of the family counseling together.

Dear reader, how do you perceive major decisions, and how do you resolve the issues? Sometimes, major decisions split families apart, or bring a togetherness of unity that becomes a real blessing. If there are problems and major issues in your family, try a family-time night to pray for guidance and hash out the issues. "Trust in the LORD with all your heart and lean not on your own understanding; in all your ways acknowledge him, and he will make your paths straight" (Proverbs 3:5–6).

Our Leaman family, with four boys and a girl, struggled in mind and spirit as we contemplated such a move. Jay, the oldest, was attending EMC. Carl, the second oldest, was at Hesston College in Hesston Kansas, and Stephen was about to begin his freshman year at EMC. Naomi (our only daughter) was an eighth-grade student at Waterman School in Harrisonburg, and Paul Jr. was a student at Pleasant Valley Elementary School.

We parents were open to the Lord's leading and faced some real questions. After I graduated from seminary, should I take a full-time pastorate somewhere in Virginia or another part of the country, or should I take the position of Administrator at the Old People's Home at Oreville in Lancaster (later called Mennonite Home)? We faced the question many times and wondered: *What direction is the Lord leading?* It was a big decision: *to go or not to go!* We began processing the matter with conversation between husband and wife, and later we held several family counseling sessions, where the children had input, too.

Our whole family talked about and discussed the proposal from Mennonite Home. The children, ten to twenty years old, were deeply involved in school and college. One evening as we were having our family counseling time, they must have counseled together in a conspiracy to boycott the idea of a move. Anyhow, in one united chorus they said, "Why move to Lancaster? Who wants to go to Pennsylvania? We don't know anyone up there?"

In a sense, some of what they blurted out in a united chorus was true. But on the other hand, they did have grandpas and grandmas living up there, and many uncles and aunts, with a sprinkling of cousins. However, at this stage in life, their view focused on school friends, whom they already knew, and they certainly were not anywhere close to dealing with "old people."

So, we continued to have family time for discussions and decision making. We would take a large pad of yellow paper and make two columns, one labeled *Pro's* and the other *Con's*. The first column was for moving to Pennsylvania for the job at Mennonite Home, and the second for pastoring a congregation. The discussion centered on our desire to see the children finish school and college in the area and my wish to finish seminary, requiring two more years in Harrisonburg.

We all realized that taking a pastorate could mean more moving around in the future because Mennonite congregations were beginning to change pastors about every five to six years in some areas. We had moved enough already in the past ten years, and none of us relished too many more moves in the next umpteen years. On the other hand, if I took the administrative job at Mennonite Home, it could be a long-term proposition if all would go well with my work. "What is the best course to take?" we asked.

After prayer and many discussions with the family, I wrote another letter to the chair of the Human Relations Committee at Mennonite Home and stated: "While it is a very noble work, we are declining the job offer at present because our children are in school, and I want to finish my graduate work at the seminary."

The board was disappointed with my answer and was hoping to find a replacement by the summer of 1974, or no later than the summer of 1975. They continued to search for another prospective Administrator. Sometime in the early part of 1975, we had an occasion to visit Lancaster. Once more a board member from Mennonite Home approached me, asking if I would reconsider and be available by June 1975. Again, our family shared counsel together and started thinking of how such a move might affect the plans of the children, and what would be the advantages and disadvantages of such a relocation at the time the Board was requesting.

What does it take to be an Administrator? I was finding out some of the implications as Erma and I tried to coordinate the thoughts of our children, sort through the likes and dislikes of our own interests, and yet give a definite answer to the Mennonite Home Human Relations Committee. It was not an easy task, but dear reader, we had God on our side, who promises in his Word never to leave us or forsake us (Deuteronomy 31:6). That is one assurance we had to help us work through this big hurdle at this stage of our lives.

For Erma and me, moving to Pennsylvania would be like going back home, since we both were born and grew up in Lancaster County. However, our children had lived in that area only a short time, and during their younger years. Now they were making lifetime friends in Virginia. Jay, Carl, and Steve were each already dating and were in the process of finding their lifelong companion. Our family jointly decided that we would not be ready to move until the spring or summer of 1976. To move any time before that was too soon for me to complete my seminary training and for the children's involvements.

We also decided that this was our final decision on dates to make a move, and that if this did not work with the Mennonite Home Board's schedule to hire a new Administrator, so be it! As a family we were 98.9 percent agreed on this time line. Therefore, I sent a letter to the chair of the Human Relations Committee, stating that June of 1975 was too soon, considering all that was involved. The summer of 1976 would be more realistic for us as a family.

This decision to stay in Harrisonburg until 1976 would let me finish my program at the seminary, to be prepared for a pastorate if God would be calling us in that direction. By the summer of 1976, the three older children would be on their way with life plans and could stay in college till they had that completed and were able to graduate.

The two younger ones, however, raised their voices in protest: "Dad and Mom, we already have our friends here, and we don't know anyone up there. Who wants to go where there are all old people?"

"Not me," said Paul Jr., and his sister chimed in immediately, "and not me either."

Now what were we to do as parents? As I reflect back on these experiences, perhaps the Lord was already testing me, to prepare me for tasks ahead at Mennonite Home, if the Board invited me again when I might be available. There are times in any organization when opposition arises to an administrative decision. In exercising the gift of administration, a true servant of the Lord must do what is best for the most and not just the few, be they residents or employees. I found guidance in meditating on Romans 12:6–8.

We parents assured these teenagers that new friendships would be available at the new school they would attend in Pennsylvania. We asked them to try to be positive about the move if we received an authorized invitation from the Mennonite Home Board. We as parents were confident that the Lord God would help us as a family through the difficult times and not leave us alone. We agreed that we are in this together! Praise the Lord, for he has said, "Never will I leave you; never will I forsake you" (Hebrews 13:5).

Eventually we agreed that, if the Mennonite Home Board would meet our time schedule, we could make the transition by June 1976. This decision gave me the assurance to answer in the affirmative. However, I did have a lingering call in my mind to be in a pastoral ministry somewhere, after I completed seminary training.

As time moved on, we were in Lancaster again and discussed this issue with the Mennonite Home Trustees, who had scheduled an interview in prospect for this new job. The Trustees made it clear that if they hired me, I would need to give the Administrator's job top priority. In fact, they discussed this opportunity as a "ministry" in itself. As Erma and I prayed and continued to search the mind of God on these matters, we became more comfortable with our decision to be available for late spring of 1976. The Trustees did say that they favored me taking some speaking appointments in churches across the Lancaster Conference to enhance the ministry of Mennonite Home, giving it some publicity.

I also counseled with our pastor at Lindale Mennonite Church in Virginia. He said, "Paul, you will need to learn to administrate with relaxed pressure." How does one do that? Just try it. Such a style is good for the body and soul, as I found out in my attempt to do just that in the years ahead. There were failures, to be sure, but then faith and trust must kick in to fill out the equation, and we move on!

The next item on the agenda was to write my letter of resignation to the principal of EMHS, where I was just completing four years of service, hard work, and some fun in raising money. I had already talked to the principal about the opportunity for me in Lancaster, but every job requires an application to be hired, and later a commendable way to terminate. This was going to be difficult. I loved this job, the "boss," and the colleagues with whom I worked. As they learned of our interests in going to Lancaster, their assuring comments and kind words on my involvement with them at the school made it all the more traumatic.

One day I sat down at my desk to write the letter of resignation. I didn't know how to start. It was frustrating, and I cried as I started again in the privacy of my office, with the door shut. Some tears dropped on the paper, making a smudge. *Oh well, it's not the end of the world! No big deal.* Yet it really was, so I finally wrote my thoughts down, what I planned to do, where I was going, and why. The why was not any negative thought about EMHS or its personnel, but about a new challenge. It was not really a big surprise to the principal, but somewhat expected as new challenges come to others to move on. The last day on the job there blessed me, with the wonderful send-off the school provided for me. Praise the Lord for his goodness and care in the pilgrimage of life.

Mennonite Home Board names Administrator: Paul G. Leaman appointed Administrator of the facility at 1520 Harrisburg Pike, Lancaster, Pa. The announcement comes one day after the unveiling of a $3.25-million remodeling project for the Home. His duties begin July 1, 1976.

Chapter 13

The Move to a New Job

The Board of Trustees agreed to wait till July 1, 1976, but no longer for a new Administrator to be on the job. It was now late summer of 1975, and the Board of Mennonite Home anticipated our meetings with them to become better acquainted. During these sessions on several trips to Lancaster, I received some orientation from the Board's perspective, and all the while I was developing enthusiasm for the new challenge. I must admit that I did not know much about the elderly at that time, and I felt quite inadequate for going into this type of ministry.

However, during this transition and preparation time, the Lord provided again. I discovered that James Madison University (JMU), in Harrisonburg, was offering several summer courses on gerontology. On one of our early visits, I mentioned this to the Board at Mennonite Home, and they suggested that I take several courses there, before our move to Lancaster. The Board offered to pay the tuition and books required to take these courses. So, back to summer school I went in 1975, even before finishing my graduate work at the seminary, projected for May 1976.

Each spring the Lancaster Conference sponsored a Capital Campaign program to raise money for conference agencies for building projects. Mennonite Home participated in this program because it needed funds to renovate or build new, since buildings at Mennonite Home were outdated. The Board asked me to attend these evening meetings three times each spring of the years 1975 and 1976, to become familiar with their process of raising money. The Board reimbursed me for my travel expense to attend these meetings in Lancaster. It really was more orientation to Lancaster people, giving me a chance to get acquainted with volunteers who solicited for building funds in their respective congregations.

All this made a very busy schedule, EMHS development work, finishing up seminary work, gerontology courses at JMU, and driving to Lancaster three times each spring for late-night meetings. *What am I getting in for? Is this really what I want to do?* The involvement was quite intense and real, and the challenge was only to go forward and not retreat.

During March of 1976, we decided that with all things going well so far, we might as well look for housing near Mennonite Home, because this involvement could well be a long-term investment of our lives. We sought a suitable house for our family of now the two youngest children and Erma and me. Two of the oldest sons were in college, living in a trailer near the EMC campus, and the second son was a dorm student at Hesston College. We finally found a nice split-level house in the Belair Development, only three street miles to Mennonite Home.

We moved from Virginia on June 5, 1976, and then took two weeks to paint, replace carpet, and make a few other changes to fit our family's lifestyle. The Lord blessed our family with newfound friends in the Lancaster area who helped us make the move and get settled in our living quarters.

As I visited Mennonite Home for short sessions with the current Administrator, residents and friends asked when I was going to move into the Home. My answer was, "We do not plan to live in the facility." I was the first administrator coming into this new job and not moving in. All previous administrators, superintendents, or stewards, as they were variously called, always lived in the facility for the previous seventy-three years of the Home's existence. I am sure some folks wondered if this new young administrator knew what he was up to. How could he run a place like this without being on call for twenty-four hours a day, and seven days a week? Nowadays, people call this a 24/7 schedule.

During the middle weeks of June 1976, I visited the Home several times, to chat with the incumbent administrator and to prepare myself for the first day on the job, which was set for July 1, 1976. My involvement actually began on June 25, 1976, when I went to a Central Pennsylvania Association of Non-profit Homes for the Aging (CENPANPHA). It met at Quarryville Presbyterian Home and was on Medicaid reimbursements. I came away from those two-day meetings rather frustrated with all the talk about Medicaid, per-diem rates, and a heap of other regulations that operators of a nursing home had to meet. As I became more deeply involved in the work, I soon learned what all those terms meant. Wow! This was not like being a development director for a high school in Virginia. I even thought, *Being a pastor in a congregation of faithful and willing people somewhere would certainly be much easier.*

Soon after we were settled in our new location, with the two youngest in school, Erma took a job in the dietary department at Brethren Village near Lititz. She soon made friends there and enjoyed her work as "first" cook, requiring a schedule from 6:00 a.m. to 2:30 p.m. five days a week, including a shift every other weekend. There was a need for kitchen help at Mennonite Home when I started there, and the administrator's wife (by tradition) had served as matron in the Home. However, my training in several courses in college suggested that an organization should avoid nepotism: "favoritism shown to a relative by giving an appointive job on a basis of relationship" (*Webster's Seventh New Collegiate Dictionary*).

Before coming to Mennonite Home, I had resolved in my mind not to hire my own family, simply to avoid any embarrassing situations that could arise inadvertently. This was an unwritten policy that I had cleared with the Board in the beginning of my employment. Since the Board did not have such a policy on the books, nor was it a historical practice, they conceded to the fact that my unwritten policy was indeed worth a try. Previously, every steward or superintendent had their spouse involved in some capacity.

From the beginning of my term, another significant change was the question of living in the facility for a 24/7 schedule. But we had two teenage children still at home, and we wanted to give them the freedom of their own wishes on the subject. Hence, we proposed to the Board early in the discussions that we would not live in the facility. Most of the Board members agreed to our plan, so I knew from early on that the Board might just be a good group to work with.

However, when the word of this decision reached the residents, many of them did not agree too well with it. One day while I was in the hallway right outside my office door, a retired minister's elderly wife met me quite abruptly as she was exiting the elevator. She stopped in the hallway about a foot in front of me and said, "So you are the new Administrator," making her head go up and down while looking me over from head to foot. She took special notice of the nice long tie I was wearing and continued her speech: "So you think you're too young to live in here with us old people. Well, I hope you will do all right, but you should live in here to take care of things right."

Wow! What am I to reply? I thought fast and suggested: "We [the Board and I] will try it this way [not living in] and see how it works. I wish especially for your prayers, and all the praying residents, on my behalf for the job ahead.

"Alright, I'll pray for you, because you certainly will need lots of it" was her kind response.

Chapter 14

Adjusting to a New Job

Just before getting into the full swing of on-the-job training, the Human Relations Committee chair handed me a job description, outlining my duties as the new administrator. I was to do the hiring, relate to the department personnel, in Nursing, Dietary, Housekeeping, Maintenance, Laundry, and the Office. Another major area was to admit new residents when a vacancy occurred, and to be a social contact if and when any problems developed between residents and/or employees. In addition, I was to relate to the president of the Board as needed, look for opportunities to help would-be donors to "unload" some of their cash to Mennonite Home, to assist in our upcoming building program.

I wasn't long at Mennonite Home till I realized that this job was much bigger and different than the one I just left a few months ago at EMHS in Harrisonburg, Virginia. This position would require many bushels of patience, wisdom, and know-how to work and manage a houseful of a hundred elderly people and fifty employees who wanted good benefits, working conditions, and more than enough money in their paychecks to just barely get by. The residents thought, talked, and walked much slower than the young people in the high school. Would I be able to make the shift?

Even the Trustees were in the elderly bracket except for three close to my own age (forty-three when I took the job), and one was significantly younger. The Board was a good mix of businessmen, farmers, and one attorney. Roy Bomberger was Board president when I began there. He was a very accommodating trustee, and I found him easy to relate to when I had questions between regular board meetings.

To learn my new job, however, I was to answer to the incumbent administrator, Henry Tyson. So exactly what was I to do, today and tomorrow? I had always been a quite work-oriented person, with a strong work ethic that required me to be busy or feel guilty for not earning my keep. My prayer to God on a daily basis was for wisdom and divine guidance for help to meet the challenges of this new job.

During the first several weeks of floundering on the job, I wondered what I was supposed to be doing. One day Henry Tyson gave me the task of gathering bids from local milk processing companies and obtaining a low bid to buy milk for the dietary department during the next year. They delivered the milk to the Home about every two weeks. The two walk-in refrigerators did a good job of keeping it cold and fresh. However, the bids and purchase for the baloney and eggs was the job of Henry, so the Dietary Department director always had to ask him to order those food staples as needed.

On the job, I also walked through the building, chatted with residents, became familiar with who they were, listened to stories of their past life, and heard that they were glad to have me on the job. However, they also let me know that one of their biggest fears was "running out of money" and suffering more aches and pains. The employees shared some of their significant frustrations with out-of-date equipment, and a few even mentioned the same concern about administration personnel. Wow, if that is the case, what can anyone do about it? I was to be in charge but was not yet in charge, and I did not yet know how to become in charge, except to do what I was told. After all, Henry had sixteen years of experience under his belt, and I had some formal education on how to do things but not yet the open door to do them.

The department heads were asking for opportunities to work and converse with me, the incoming administrator. Since there was limited office space, Henry and I shared the same office for six to eight months. We had the understanding that when he needed the office for a private interview with someone, I would go out on the floors and become better acquainted with the facility, residents, and employees. Other than me taking bids for the milk and Henry buying the baloney and cheese, I didn't have much work in an official manner. To say the least, I was frustrated.

Many times I wondered why I ever took this job. Some of my frustrations were of my own making, not being prepared for how slow a system of changeover can be. Several times I was so discouraged that my thoughts deeply affected me emotionally. Sometimes I was so discouraged that I went into the men's room and literally cried my heart out to the walls. Then I washed my face with cold water and hoped the redness of my eyes and nose would quickly go away. I felt as though I shouldn't stay in the men's room too long or others in the office might wonder, *Where is that new young administrator? What does he think he's doing, not staying on the job?* After as much time elapsed as I felt comfortable with, I went back into the office to see what Henry wanted me to do next in this orientation time.

In those days the maintenance person also had the title of Assistant Administrator, with Henry bearing the title of Administrator. The employees came to know me as an Associate Administrator.

Chapter 15

Rescued, Just in Time

I was now almost eight weeks on the job, and department directors were asking when I was going to be in charge. I didn't know and wished I did have some direction. As I reflect back now, I must give the incumbent the credit of having worked there nearly sixteen years. The work and organization had ingrained themselves into his system well. But he was getting to be elderly. Wouldn't he want to give up some pressure and responsibility? Nevertheless, he didn't talk about the matter, and so the days dragged on for me, with him still in charge.

One day the chair of the Human Relations Committee stopped by, took me aside, and asked, "How are things going?" I shared my frustrations, not having any definite direction on how to be in charge or to be involved significantly in the operation. He took the concerns back to his committee and the Board. The Trustees decided to have a department turned over to my responsibility every forty-five days until all were transferred. It was now mid-September 1976, and the plan was to begin October 1, only two weeks later.

About that time, the local Farmers Home Administration (FHA) asked for an updated financial profile for a loan application, which was in the works for more than two years, waiting on government approval. This application was to obtain a low-interest loan from the Farmer's Home Administration in Washington, DC, with offices in Harrisburg and Lancaster, to put up a replacement building since the current structure was condemned under the Life Safety Code for a nursing home.

After Henry looked at the request for an updated financial report, he told me he did not have a clue what they wanted. "Would you look at it?"

I readily agreed to do that. I perused the multitude of pages for several hours and finally got the drift of what was involved. It was a financial projection for the operation, and they wanted it updated to show what things might look like during the first five years after we opened the new building. I was fairly proficient with figures, so Henry asked me to do what I could with it. After digging into the financial records of the Home, and comparing the current with the projected report (now about three years old), I had a feel for what the FHA wanted. As a result, we updated, retyped, and submitted the projection to Harrisburg and Washington. To the surprise of Henry and me, the report was accepted. In the process, I learned a lot. It showed me firsthand what we could expect from the operation if the FHA ever approved this new building loan application.

The new Administrator, hard at work updating information for the financial statements.

The approval came to me via a phone call from Representative Eshleman, from the Lancaster office the day before Christmas in 1976. He said, "Merry Christmas, Mr. Leaman, and I am most pleased to tell you the loan has been approved in Washington, and the papers will be ready to sign by January 4, 1977." This was the best news for Mennonite Home, and the beginning of an unending building program for years to come. Praise the Lord! God is good, providing for our spiritual needs through Jesus Christ, but also for the material needs, for funds to continue the ministry of caring for the elderly.

Now things were looking up for my new job. The question in mind was, *How will this mandated transition go?* There were seven departments to be transferred: Nursing, Dietary, Maintenance, Housekeeping, Laundry, Activities, and Office. Which one would come first? Henry didn't say anything to me about the transition till two days before the date to turn over the first department. It was September 29, 1976, and nothing changed. In fact, he replied to my query, "It's not time yet." So at about 5:00 p.m. on September 30, I again asked Henry about the change. He said, "Which department do you want?"

Grace Supplee, registered nurse (RN), Director of Nursing, had asked that if I had a choice, she wanted me to ask for her department. So I did, and Henry replied, "Well, you took the biggest one first." My thought was, *So be it. We have to start somewhere.* Forty-five days later, Henry and I agreed that the second department he would put in my care should be Dietary; these two departments had to work together rather closely due to special diets for nursing care residents. Henry turned over all other departments smoothly, one by one, till the allotted time transpired.

Chapter 16

Organizational Responsibility

Now that the operation was in my responsibility, I felt an urgent need to bring unity and cohesiveness to the various departments. It became clear that the department directors were asking for the same thing to happen, so that greater coordination could develop on the level in which each respective department had to interrelate to each other. We decided to meet each Wednesday morning at 8:30 a.m., in the small basement dining room outside the laundry. I encouraged all directors to be prompt. The meetings went well for several weeks, and the directors were doing well on promptness.

The department directors meetings helped me tremendously to become acquainted with the seven departments and gather a good feel for their needs and the struggles and challenges facing an old facility. We anticipated a new building in the near future. The directors meetings also did wonders to keep them abreast of developments in the new building plans, with opportunities to share the blueprints in staff meetings, explaining how this *big* project was going to impact their work and schedules.

One Wednesday morning Verna Sauder, the Food Service Director, and Grace Supplee, RN, Director of Nursing were ten or so minutes late. We waited at least five minutes, but then went on without them rather than delay all the others, who had pressing schedules to keep. We usually began our meetings with a special prayer time, and requests. Just as we finished prayer time, the door opened, and in burst the two absent directors. Grace quickly said, "Sorry we are late, but we just had a delivery in the Nursing Department, and I needed Verna to help because the incident had to do with her department."

What, is she a midwife and able to practice, and no one knew her skills other than dietary? we thought as we burst out laughing for several minutes, just knocking my train of thought off the tracks. Questions were racing through a few heads: *Wow, what is this place coming to? A delivery in the Nursing Department among those elderly people? Who is it? What happened? Did everything go alright?*

Grace Supplee quickly said, "No it wasn't what you may have first thought, the way I burst out with my statement. We had a shipment of a special dietary supplement for the Dietary Department, which we will eventually use in my department, but the driver took it to the wrong place. It belongs in the kitchen pantry first, and then we take it as needed to the Nursing Department." We were all relieved: no special announcement would be necessary about the episode. It sure helped to break the ice in a directors meeting that was getting started, and with a new administrator at that.

Chapter 17

Scared but Not Hurt

One cold blustery and wintry night in January 1977, I received a phone call from the Home to come over right away. It was 12:30 to 1:00 a.m. What could be wrong now? I lived three miles away, and Henry was still living in a ground-floor residential room facing the creek, on the south side of the building. I hurriedly dressed and drove to the Home in about three minutes, record time! At that time of the night, hardly a car was in sight, and happily I did not meet a trooper in his squad car.

As I was speeding down the road to the Route 30 bypass, I heard a fire truck siren wailing in the distance. Were they heading for Mennonite Home? Sure enough, as I approached the driveway at 1520 Harrisburg Pike, the fire truck was at the front entrance, with fireman getting out of the truck and hurrying into the facility. I parked off to the side and also went in the front entrance. I was quickly directed to the ground floor and to the old furnace room, where Henry was. He looked rather worried and a little haggard from the stress he was under.

I quickly asked, "What happened? Is there something I should be doing?" By then, the firemen were in control.

As it happened, one of the old oil burners blew up, and the fire from the exploding burner lit the fuel oil that had spilled on the floor. The fuel oil was burning and gaining momentum as the flames became larger, spreading over the furnace room floor. Henry had it almost under control with a fire extinguisher by the time the firemen arrived. The firemen soon had it completely extinguished. They used large fans to exhaust the black smoke and the odor of burning fuel oil out of the building.

The scary part of the episode was the fire to start with. In addition, the safety of the residents was our utmost concern. We on staff had the residents evacuated to safety to "play it safe" for their benefit. Another scary part of the experience was that the building was so old and dry, with a brick veneer over wood framing. If the fire would have gotten out of control, flames would have engulfed the whole building in a few minutes. Residents could have lost their lives, perhaps, not to mention the equipment, furniture, business records, and the entire building. Thank God there was a team effort on the part of the firemen, the staff, and the quick response of Henry Tyson, who lived in the facility.

This episode certainly raised the issue of the new young Administrator not living in the facility. Some residents asked, "Now just how would you handle such a situation if it would happen when you [Paul] are in charge and don't have Henry living there to fall back on?"

It was a valid argument on their part. As yet, I was not completely in charge and allowed to exercise my style of management in all kinds of situations. However, it did promote quite serious thinking on my part, and some necessary discussion at the next Board meeting. We were all thankful to God for the safety and teamwork that occurred in that emergency; no one got hurt or burned or was left homeless. The repairmen from E. H. Gochnauer and Sons responded promptly to our service call, repaired the faulty burner, checked all the systems out, and declared it safe again to use.

We gave much thought to this issue before the next Board meeting so that I could intelligently answer how I would handle the future safety of the residents after I would be in charge. The older men on the Board (except the President) had strong opinions in favor of requiring the new Administrator to live in the Home.

From a management standpoint, my answer to the situation was eventually to have a night watchman on duty to care for such situations and keep an eye on all the equipment, to facilitate a smooth operation in case of a breakdown. As an interim provision, we also discussed giving the night-shift Nursing Supervisor the authority to call the Fire Department or the Administrator until a better system was in place. There was no finger-pointing toward anyone, but this discussion seemed to satisfy the concerns for the time being. After all, a new building was in the works, and then we would modernize the fire alarm system anyway.

This experience and my later reflection on it (in March 2006) remind me of the words of the songwriter Kittie Louise Suffield:

> *God is still on his throne,*
> *and he will remember his own;*
> *tho' trials may press and burdens distress us,*
> *he never will leave us alone.*
>
> *God is still on the throne,*
> *he never forsaketh his own,*
> *his promise is true, he will not forget you,*
> *God is still on his throne.*

Chapter 18

A New Building in the Making

The big roll of blueprints had been in the closet too long. Now it was time to get them out for review. The local architect firm of Hauck, Kauffman, Reese, and Beers spent a good deal of time reviewing the blueprints, to be sure all requirements of the Life Safety Code were up-to-date. The firm prepared the bidding documents for contractors to bid on this project for Mennonite Home. At an estimated cost of 3.1 million dollars, it was a huge undertaking for the organization. Eight contractors bid on the project. The successful low bidder was Wickersham Construction of Lancaster. This was making history and becoming a story as part of these memoirs. Appropriate Board members signed a contract on May 25, 1977, in the law offices of Wenger, Byler, & Thomas, in Lancaster's center square.

Not only was I overwhelmed with concern for this big task of a new building project; I also was learning the procedures of operating a nursing home. I was in the midst of reading, studying various materials, and listening to tapes in preparation to take the state board exam in Harrisburg, to acquire a Nursing Home Administrator (NHA) license. In this job there was no such thing as an eight-hour day, but more like ten- to fourteen-hour days. But I was looking ahead to taking the state boards and becoming certified.

After an appointment, and a trip to Harrisburg about the same week the Board signed a contract for the new building, Roy Bomberger and I met the appropriate officials in the Occupational Licensing Bureau for my temporary NHA license. They granted it without a problem. Now I was recognized as the Administrator in charge. Actually, by this time I had all departments in my responsibility. Within a few months Henry and Eva Tyson moved out of the Home to a house in Neffsville. I could tell it was a tough move for them both, but that's the way life is sometimes. After serving for one year as a licensed Administrator, I was eligible to take the written state boards for the permanent NHA license. In the fall of 1977, I managed to pass the tough examination on the first try.

We held the groundbreaking ceremonies for the new building on Saturday, May 28, 1977, at 10:30 a.m. It was a gorgeous spring day. Excitement, anticipation, and wonderment prevailed among all who attended, especially the residents. They threw concerned questions at me, for example wondering, "What will this big expenditure do to my room rates?" Construction began on May 31, 1977, with a two-year contract for the building to be completed. The contractor did a superb job, completing the project under the two-year contract, allowing staff and volunteers to move from the old building into the new on May 23, 1979.

It was a joyous day, the talk and intermingling of volunteers and residents as they with their families walked the long hallway between the old and the new to their new rooms. Their happy smiles and faces were a real boost for all as we shared together this momentous event. However, just when I thought everyone on staff was happy, the very morning of the move, I received a knock on my office door. It was the head RN in charge of the skilled area of fifty-one nursing residents.

She was quick about it: she handed me her letter of resignation and simply said, "That is the way I feel about it, so good-bye, and I wish you well." What a blow! Within two months, the Director of Nursing (DON), handed in her resignation, and so did the two Activities personnel. These were serious blows to my plans for getting things going. My thinking was that the new building would greatly satisfy staff, providing more modern equipment and other amenities.

In my later reflection, perhaps they needed a change, just as administration needed a change. I wondered if they didn't like what I was doing or how I was trying to run the Home. I certainly thanked the good Lord for those who stayed on the job, putting their shoulder to the wheel (so to speak), and pulled their share of the load. But these events still baffled me. Didn't they like me? I wanted everyone to like me as a person, and as their Administrator, including the residents.

After nursing my own wounds for several weeks and praying much about these matters, I confided with a trustee who was secretary on the Board. He gave me some good counsel and advice: "Paul, you are not going to please everybody here, no matter how hard you try. So do what is best for the most. Follow board policies and decisions, and do the best you can for all cases in between." That was sound counsel, and from that day on, his advice helped me to develop my way of administrating.

Chapter 19

Change, Change, and More Changes

When I started working at Mennonite Home, a fine Christian young lady (Loretta Metzler) was the receptionist in the front office. Loretta was thorough in her work, pleasant, but just a bit shy at times, yet very friendly as she flashed a gorgeous smile. She certainly became an attractive lady for a young man living not too distant. After some serious dating time, he asked for her hand in marriage, so they could share their lives together. Sure enough, she handed in her one-month resignation notice. After I put an advertisement in the local conference newsletter, several competent young ladies applied. After several interviews with the applicants, I offered Karen E. Bauman the job. She began working in June 1977, serving as receptionist-secretary in the front office.

The typewriter in the office was quite old and worn out. It was difficult to do professional typing with the old machine, so I asked the Board to approve a new one. The IBM company brought in a new eight-hundred-dollar Selectric machine to try for a week. After a week of use, we all left work for the weekend, with the new demonstrator typewriter on Karen's desk. Monday morning, after Karen came to work, she was about to do some typing for me, and lo, the new typewriter was not on her desk.

She came to my office door, knocked, opened it, and asked, "Paul, where is the new typewriter? It is not on my desk."

I replied, "I don't know. It was there when I left about 6:00 p.m. on Friday night." I called the IBM salesman and told him the story. He was as baffled as we were. To this day, I have never heard what became of that new typewriter. However, we (the

Board and office personnel) knew the facility was vulnerable: we never locked the facility except for the Administrator's office door and the medication cabinet at the nurses' station.

So we initiated another change that same day. I informed the Board President of the incident, and that very evening I began to lock all outside doors by 9:30 p.m., and unlock them by 6:00 a.m. each day, seven days a week. Though I lived only three miles away, it still became an extra nuisance to go there twice a day to lock and unlock. At the next Board meeting, I asked for permission to hire a night watchman to be on duty from 10:00 p.m. till 6:00 a.m. seven days a week. It actually took two part-time employees to fill the schedule.

This schedule worked well. In fact, that summer we hired an experienced person to take a five-day shift. We approved the application from Henry Tyson now that he and Eva (his wife) had moved to Neffsville, to the house they had bought. This arrangement worked for about a year. Then Eva Tyson, while visiting some resident friends one day, said to me, "Paul, could you find someone else to take Henry's place on night shift? He's working too hard for his age." I assured her I would, provided I received his resignation letter stating that he wanted to terminate. A few days later that letter came. I hired a new employee to fill the gap.

Time out for a game of pool by Administrator Paul Leaman and his father, Sanford D. Leaman, resident. The competition was keen, with Father Leaman winning two rounds out of three played. 1980 photo.

A New Maintenance Supervisor

Now that Phares Kemrer had fully retired, it was time to recruit a new maintenance supervisor. The time was September 1978, so after some advertising by word of mouth and the conference newsletter, a recently retired farmer came by and applied for the job. Henry Leaman had a farm along the Strasburg Pike, and now his son was on the farm. He was ready to take on a new challenge, and the timing was right since he could learn the new systems as the new building was being built.

Henry was a likeable person to be on staff. He could get along well with residents, fix things for them, and in general was a good mechanic. He also could tell jokes now and then, making the day go by swiftly for some. Henry could handle Lloyd Rohrer's personality quite well. Lloyd was a very hard worker and took care of trash disposal, newspapers, and many other tasks too numerous to mention.

Henry's skills saved the Home many dollars in maintenance costs when he could fix things without calling in a plumbing or electrical firm to do the job. Many times Henry could fix something the same day, when outside professionals perhaps couldn't come for several days due to their busy schedules.

Changing the Old Building

The new building, known as Parkvue, was finished and occupied by May 23, 1979. Then, due to Life Safety Code, we had to deal with the old original structure. Renovation plans called for removing two top floors of the original building, installing a new flat roof, and gutting the inside to bring the structure up to code.

I remember the excitement we had in traipsing through mounds of dirt at times, while still trying to maintain a clean and safe environment for residents and employees. We constructed a long closed-in temporary hallway to get from the old building to the annex, north-south wing, and the east wing. There was more dirt and debris and inconveniences, but we all knew that it would get worse before it got better. However, it finally did get better, and what a day of rejoicing that was.

Chapter 20

Stories of Residents

Humorous Phares

Phares Kemrer, an older Home employee, had an interesting personality. He was a good man to talk to about the changes coming to Mennonite Home and the transition of Administrators. He advised, "Paul, change will come. Just stay around and do what you can. We are just as eager for changes as you are. It will take some time, so hang in there."

So, I decided to hang in there, learn all I could while treading water, so to speak. At first I ordered more milk as needed, while Henry ordered the cheese and baloney for the Dietary Department. As I reflect on this practice now, it seems rather funny. The way the system was run seemed "full of baloney." Anyway, the residents got their milk, eggs, and baloney because the Administrators were ordering it.

Phares continued to take me under his wing, mentoring me for the job just like the apostle Paul did for the young man Timothy (see Paul's mentoring in 1 and 2 Timothy and Titus). One day Phares took me on a tour of the building to explain the oil burners in the basement furnace room. They were old and enclosed in a fireproof room. As he described the old system, he remarked, "I hope they never blow up; this building is a real fire-trap."

The thing we feared did happen. One night a furnace blew up and ignited some fuel oil on the floor within the fireproof room. Henry Tyson called the fire department but also used the fire extinguishers to put out the blaze before the fire truck arrived. He called me, and I rushed to the Home. It was a scary experience because the building was so old and could have quickly burned if the fire had gotten outside the furnace room. We prayed and thanked the good Lord for the residents' safety and that the building was saved (see chapter 17).

Phares Kemrer was one faithful employee who stayed around for about a year even after Henry left the office for his retirement. Phares was in charge of maintenance and also assisted in the laundry, to keep the old machines running in that department.

He was a quite congenial person, with a keen sense of humor. One day he came into my office and shared a story: "Paul, I'll bet you can't guess what I saw today?" He had that usual "twinkle" in his eye, and I knew he had a joke up his sleeve, but what was it?

"I was walking around the grounds checking the shrubbery along the walk, out here by the back door, and saw this white piece of paper lying on the walk. I was about to pick it up when I noticed a 'black streak' across the paper, and it looked as though it was moving. *That's strange,* I thought, so I looked closer and saw that it was a short letter with a coupon on the bottom that one could separate from the main letter. And you know what, Paul? In fine print I read, 'Tear across here.' You know what it was? A multitude of little black ants were running back and forth along this dotted line above the coupon. They were tearing across here just as the message said. Now don't you think they were smart ants?"

What could I say? After the suspense of the joke dawned on me, we both had a hardy laugh. Did you have a hearty laugh after reading this story? I hope so! Look up and read Psalm 126:2 and Proverbs 17:22: "A merry heart does good like a medicine" (KJV).

His colleagues and the residents liked Phares for his amicable and honest way of life. Eventually he decided to retire and spend more time on his hobby of woodworking, in his shop at home. He salvaged some lumber from the old barn just west of the Home, cut the pieces to the size he wanted, and turned out some beautiful rose vases on his wood lathe.

This led to further orientation on the job. Phares was in charge to see that the Home did the fire drills (required by Labor and Industry) on a timely basis each month, and on all three shifts: 7:00 a.m. to 3:00 p.m., 3:00 p.m. to 11:00 p.m., and 11:00 p.m. to 7:00 a.m. One night soon after the fire scare with the furnace, Phares and I went in during the graveyard shift, between 11:00 p.m. and midnight. Three nurses were on duty for the fifty-one nursing beds at that time. Most of the residents were sleeping, and the employees were not too busy, so we had some time to get acquainted. Not much activity was happening, and things seemed to be quite dead. "It sure seems to be the graveyard shift," I commented. "What do you do at night?" I asked the supervisor.

"Oh, we eat, potty those who must go, and give meds as required," she said. "But Paul, if you think this is a rather dead graveyard shift, you need to come in here when it is full moon. It is very much alive as these people get hyper, won't sleep, and try to get up when they should stay in bed.

"Sure sounds exciting to work here," I replied. "How do you like it?"

"Oh, we love it here. There are so many good residents who need us every day. It makes coming to work exciting and worthwhile."

After about an hour at the facility, Phares and I went home. I tried to go back to sleep, but it was difficult. Lots of thoughts were going through my head, and I was thinking, *This must be a good place to work after all, if I could only be in charge.* Phares's words kept ringing in my ears, "Hang in there, Paul. Change will come, but it moves slow." I guess that meant another bushel of patience for me to feed on.

Shine: A Unique Personality

After I had served for a little less than a year, residents were beginning to know my openness to any stories they might have, and that I would even take time to listen. As residents left the dining room, many would walk past my office to reach their rooms. One morning a resident by the name of Carrie Siple from Wrightsville, Pennsylvania, stopped by Karen's desk and asked if she could see Mr. Leaman. Karen checked if I was busy and told me that "Shine" wanted to see me. Shine was her nickname, used more than Carrie because she really did "shine" in her spirit and on her smiling face. Shine was seventy-nine years old in 1976. She was born August 4, 1897; admitted to the Home on April 4, 1973; and died March 3, 1988, after a full and joyful life.

I met her in the hallway just outside my office door. She said, "Oh, Mr. Leaman, I am so glad to see you. I have something I must tell you." She would stop by frequently to bring me up-to-date on happenings and how things were from her perspective throughout the Home. "Now, Mr. Leaman," she said, "your job requires a dignified title. So, if it is alright with you, I will always call you Mr. Leaman."

"Yes, Shine," I replied, "that will be just fine."

Her reports about conditions throughout the Home were positive and upbeat, as was her personality. She was single and liked to talk about male-female relationships at times, in a wholesome way. She told me that once she had a four-year friendship with a man, and they had become engaged, but then she broke it off because he was preparing for the ministry. "Mr. Leaman, do you think I would have made a minister's wife?" Then she answered her own question: "Why, I guess not!" and really laughed, as she often did.

Shine certainly was a jolly person. One day she said, "Mr. Leaman, if I ever get into a relationship again that leads to marriage, I will have you be the lucky person to walk me down the aisle, since I have no living relatives to do the honors." What a promise and an honor, but it never did happen.

"Mr. Leaman, you know I was never married, so I am just an old maid, or as someone said, 'a leftover blessing.' I have a riddle to ask you. How are a rotten lemon and an old maid alike?"

This riddle took me off guard! I know that lemons (the fruit) are very sour, and surely a rotten one could be doubly sour. But

Shine was always such a sweet character, so it would not be anything concerning her personality. After I had been thinking several minutes, trying to solve the riddle, an audience of residents and some employees began gathering to hear the answer. I am not sure if any of them knew the right answer or not, but if they did, no one volunteered a solution just yet. I think they were trying to put me to the test and on trial to see if I was smart or a spoilsport. Finally, after trying several answers, I was getting nowhere with an answer that satisfied the inquirer. So I said, "Shine, I do not know, so ask me the riddle again."

"Mr. Leaman, how are a rotten lemon and an old maid alike? Well, neither one is worth squeezing."

How clever! She was so sweet about the riddle, and so jolly and seemed always to be in such a sweet disposition that I just had to give her a mild squeeze across the shoulders, which she deserved and liked very much. The audience of numerous residents and a few employees soon disbanded. The workers didn't want to be off duty too long and give this new Administrator wrong impressions. That is the beautiful story of Shine!

The Traffic Director

Another interesting resident was a retired railroad employee, Ralph Supplee, an elderly and rather obese individual, lived in the Home from April 10, 1973, until he died on August 26, 1985. He was legally blind, shuffled slowly in his walk, and used a cane to steady himself. This gentleman was in his mideighties when the author learned to know him. He had worked on the railroad all his life and kept a big red flag as a souvenir of his job. As memorabilia from his railroad job, he also wore blue-and-white striped denim bib overalls and owned a matching cap.

This man had an insatiable hunger for candy, which the doctor had ordered him not to eat because of his weight and diabetes. For many years a Weis Market was directly across the street from the Home, on the north side of Harrisburg Pike. When he wanted candy, he would start shuffling across the busy

Harrisburg Pike, using his big red flag to "wave down" the eastbound traffic. Once he got them to stop, he would meander across the roadway to the center turning lane and try to stop the westbound traffic, so he could walk over to Weis Market.

Once I saw both lanes of traffic stopped, with vehicles backed up beyond the traffic signal intersection. This particular day not only were cars stopped but also a big tractor trailer rig, right where Ralph was standing, and the driver was blowing his air horn continuously. The more the air horn sounded, the more vehemently Ralph waved his big red flag. It was a hilarious situation, yet also volatile and dangerous. I could see the whole scenario unfolding before my very eyes from my office window.

I am sure he wanted to exercise safety by using his flag. But he was not authorized to stop traffic on this busy highway. The motorists and especially the truck driver resented his directions. The nurses on his floor noticed him missing and began a search. When they discovered him out on the highway, they tried all means of coaxing him to return, but to no avail. That is when they called on me for assistance.

Here is the picture: Ralph in his striped bib overalls, the nurses dressed in white uniforms, and Mr. Leaman in his white shirt, suit, and tie, all out on the road trying to get Ralph back to safety. My attempts were rather fruitless when he realized that another voice of authority was trying to convince him to come back to the Home.

"Listen here, young fella," he said, "who made you a boss over me to tell me what I can and cannot do? You will not get me to go, and that is that. I am not going until I get the merchandise I need at Weis Market."

Something had to be done, so with two nurses on each side, they literally forced him to walk back off the highway to the Mennonite Home curbside. By then another group of nurses came on the scene with a wheelchair, to transport him into the facility. What a blessing to have good help and responsible employees! This looked like teamwork to me, and I congratulated the staff for their help.

In the process, I confiscated his red flag for a few minutes and used it to wave the traffic into motion again since Ralph was on the way to safety. During my first years in the office, there were several such episodes with Ralph and the staff. We discussed the situation in staff meetings. Someone suggested keeping him busy in activities and asking Social Services to give some more input regarding Ralph and his conduct. With stepped-up procedures of staff interaction, they kept Ralph busy in conduct other than directing traffic.

Spiritually Alive!

Another interesting resident was a devout Jewish Christian by the name of Hannah Sporn. She came to the Home from the Paxton Street facility operated by the Brethren in Christ Church in Harrisburg. Hannah was born on October 5, 1921, admitted to the Home on September 12, 1977, and went to her eternal reward on March 7, 1995. She was rather plump for her short height, diabetic, and walked with a wobbly gait. Hannah knew how to cross the busy Harrisburg Pike, so she would walk to Park City and buy food she should not eat because of her health problems.

The unique characteristic of this Jewish-Christian lady was her deep love for the Lord Jesus. She never feared to talk to strangers in a forthright manner about her faith in Jesus. Hannah testified about her faith in a fearless way to anyone who would give a listening ear.

Dear Friend, when out in the public, are you ever ashamed of Jesus in your daily life? The Scripture quotes Jesus' words, "If anyone is ashamed of me and my words, the Son of Man will be ashamed of him when he comes in his glory and in the glory of the Father and of the holy angels" (Luke 9:26). If you profess to be a Christian, are you ashamed to let others know you identify with Jesus with even the small action of bowing your head in prayer in a public place before eating? This practice often opens up a door to converse with others about faith values as we walk with Jesus daily.

Hannah was financially destitute and needed subsidized income from the Social Security Administration for her disabilities. She was eligible for benefits to help pay her own way at the Home. For whatever she couldn't pay, the Home absorbed the deficit in her account.

Before having a Social Service employee on staff, the Administrator had the privilege of taking her to the Social Security office. I vividly remember one particular day. Hannah point-blank asked the Social Service person if she was ready to meet Jesus and told her that, if she is not, she will end up in hell. Hannah had a clear testimony that she really believed in, yet at times her ways were embarrassing to staff who transported her among the public. She wanted to help people (no matter who it was) to become more aware of their need for a Savior. For her own spiritual enrichment, Hannah became an avid piano player and spent many hours at the piano in the chapel, tapping out the old gospel hymns that she loved so well.

Florence T. Mellinger, Caring with Compassion

A resident who gave much of her life to benefit Mennonite Home, Florence T. Mellinger was born on August 21, 1913; admitted to the Home on August 30, 1984; and went to her eternal reward on May 26, 1999. Residents and staff liked her well. She assisted whenever and wherever she could throughout the Home.

Florence was a sister to Henry S. Tyson, Administrator from 1961–76. For the years 1952–61, she was matron serving alongside Jacob D. Mellinger, whom she married in 1953. She studied, took the necessary test, and became a licensed practical nurse (LPN) in 1970. When I began serving officially on July 1, 1976, Florence eagerly welcomed this new Administrator. More than once, she offered her time and memory to the author in the transition of administrations. She had such a wealth of knowledge and experience in the facility and readily shared what she could. I am deeply indebted to her for many notes, stories, and important information to compile this book of memoirs.

Following is some warm-hearted information from Florence as the author interviewed her. First come incidents when she was matron at the Home, then as a resident, and later, as a longtime volunteer:

"How far back can you remember about Mennonite Home?"

"Paul, I can go back to the late 1920s, when I came with my parents to visit a relative, Elias Stauffer."

"What was the Home like then?"

"It was much smaller and seemed like one big family. There was always a need for good workers. Jacob D. Mellinger was superintendent (1946–61), with his wife, Lydia Sauder Mellinger, serving as matron. When Lydia met me for the first time, she told me they needed someone to work at the Home. At that time I was thirty-three years old, single (never having been married), so I decided to take the job. It was August 1946."

"What was your job?"

"I was to take the place of a general worker who had left all of a sudden, without giving notice. [Does that sound familiar?] I assisted with baths; hung out the washed clothes on the outside wash lines, where even on cold mornings the clothes would freeze stiff; cleaned residents' rooms; and assisted with tray service to the rooms."

"Florence, you mentioned the term *matron* several times, and after you were here awhile, you served as matron. What does that title mean?"

"*Matron* means 'mother' or 'to be motherly.' Most matrons are younger than the folks we have in our care. Could we not think of ourselves as daughters giving help and counsel? The best Scripture to describe the work of a matron is in Proverbs 31:10–31. I believe it is well to pattern our life after that Scripture. If only more of the young girls/ladies working today could live after that pattern.

"A matron was also a general all-around public-relations person and always had to be ready to be a 'shock absorber' when working with residents and staff. Sometimes it required being a peacemaker among residents or employees. A matron will always be a good listener, so that often the least said, the better. It is better to 'wear out' than to rust out. A good example of two women in the Bible are Mary and Martha, who showed great hospitality to Jesus (Luke 10:38–42).

"What did you like about working for Lydia Mellinger?"

"She wanted everyone to call her 'Mama Mellinger,' indicating a very close and affectionate relationship, which she really supplied! I was young and needed someone to lean on, and Lydia was that person. Then one day while working in the garden, she complained of not feeling well, and all of a sudden she died. The doctor called it a heat stroke. She was only seventy-four years of age. All of a sudden, I wondered, *Who will take the place of being the matron?* Her death was extremely hard for me. I knew the operation of the Home as well as she did, but now who could I lean on?

"Paul, it was good that I took much time to pray about this situation. As a staff worker, doing the work Mama Mellinger did, I prayed for someone on whom I could lean for support. I thought of a 'trusted' registered nurse, but none seemed to fit my need at that time. So I prayed some more. Since I was doing the work of Mama Mellinger, I was asked to sit at the same dinner table with Jacob D. Mellinger, the Superintendent. I went along with this arrangement but at times felt uncomfortable, and then at other times I really liked the privilege. In fact, in a few weeks I would notice, out of the corner of my eye, that Jacob was looking at me while we were eating at the table. Was he 'eyeing' me for some special reason? At times, it seemed like my heart would flutter with excitement over these glances.

Since in doing the work of a matron, I had to work closely with Jacob, I often got into the office to keep it clean as well as other areas. I needed someone to lean on and found Jacob to be open and ready for that kind of more intimate talks, and friendship. One day while cleaning the office, he especially mentioned to me how much he appreciated my work and understanding of the needs of residents, and his own needs due to the loss of Lydia.

Oh, did that ever make my heart flutter again! What was he saying? I never heard a man talk that way to me before."

As she told me the story of a "blossoming friendship," she would chuckle in her unique way, smile broadly, and display an expectant and tingly look all over her face.

"And Paul, then one day he really surprised me when he said, 'Florence, if I wasn't so old, . . . ,' and I knew right away what he was thinking."

Then she said, "Why, Paul, even a Board member knew what was going on and had told Jacob, 'If you decide to get married, why don't you just go ahead and do it?'

"Well, Paul, this relationship only grew to the point of getting better, both at the table, in the hallways, and when I cleaned the office. One day I thought he was going to propose to me, but instead he asked me to go with him for a walk in Long's Park, just east of Park City. These walks in the park became quite frequent. It was a pleasure for me to have him to lean on, since I never quite knew what that would be like, since I was nearing forty years of age and had never married.

"As we walked, it was comfortable for me to take his hand in mine when he offered his, and then one day he asked me if I would consent to be his wife. I was already anticipating the question, and now I thought, *He needs a wife, so what should I do? Marry him or continue as an employee?*

"Paul, I could tell he wanted me, he needed me, and I needed him. He even said that he believed the Lord kept me for him. So we told each other our thoughts. We talked some more, and finally we decided to take some time to pray more about it, and then decide within two more weeks. We soon did some more serious talking, taking long walks, and sharing ideas. We began planning a wedding and our future together.

"We married within eleven months of Mama Mellinger's passing, in April 1953. We did not have time to get away for any lengthy honeymoon, so we would go away for a long weekend several times soon after our marriage, leaving the office responsibility to a well-trusted resident. We had a good life together, and in Jacob's failing health for many years, I cared for him 24/7 as needed and as I was able. I worked as an LPN until my brother Henry Tyson became Administrator, and his wife, Eva, became the new matron.

"Paul, after thirty-five years of service to Mennonite Home, with nine of those years as Matron, I was happy to retire."

Then she said, "The most precious experience I ever received from another person, especially a man, was the tender understanding I received from my late husband, Jacob. I needed him to help me learn to be more kind. I have a tendency to be somewhat harsh. Jacob overheard me speaking impatiently with another person. . . . His respect for me caused him to remain silent. But later, he opened my Bible to Ephesians 4:32 and outlined the verse in red, leaving it open for me to find. He knew how to communicate with me kindly." She was silent for a moment, then added, "God has been good in teaching me and helping me through the rough spots."

After she shared some more reflections, she volunteered this information for the author to contemplate: "Paul, some say you tell us how to die, but not how to live in old age and retirement."

Wow, what a statement to think about! Now, as author, I am in that retirement stage of life, and have I learned to live in older age, and grow in the retirement stage, gracefully? Think about it, dear reader: life is so short! As I was growing up, we had a motto in my home with this message: "Only one life, 'twill soon be past; only what's done for Christ will last!" (missionary C. T. Studd's dying words).

The time I spent with Florence was very rewarding. Her memories go back to the early days of the 1950s, so I asked her, "Do you remember the motto inscribed on the archway inside the front door to the facility?"

"Yes, I do," she replied. "It was Psalm 37:25, 'I have been young, and now am old; yet have I not seen the righteous forsaken, nor his seed begging bread' [KJV]."

"So, Florence, what can a person do in older age?"

She told me that, after retiring, she developed a prayer list, which she used every day. She would spread it out before the Lord and pray down across her list, with praise to the Lord; then pray for government, friends, Mennonite Home, its employees, the Board, strength for the day, and for those less fortunate. Here are two poems she shared with me that meant a lot to her:

The Kneeling Camel

The camel at the close of the day,
Kneels down upon the sandy plain,
To have his burden lifted off
And rest to gain.

My soul, thou too shouldst to thy knees
When daylight draweth to a close,
And let the Master lift thy load
And grant repose.

(Anna Temple)

Old People's Home

The banks of the Little Conestoga,
near the beautiful Long's Park,
generations ago, went to and fro,
travelers by this old landmark.

Through the kindness of a brother
who was blessed with real estate
And felt grateful to another
who was not so fortunate,

His desire was to tender
space that he would designate
For the poor and homeless members,
fertile acres, six or eight.

A committee was appointed by the Districts,
twelve or more,
Individually and jointed,
opened wide Charity's door.

The indenture fixed and dated,
deed for land they occupy;
From the water's edge it started,
and surroundings high and dry.

All acknowledged the conveyance,
building sites it did convey.
With submission, no abeyance,
work commenced without delay.

A Home has now been founded,
of which we hope to write;
The principles are grounded
by the modest Mennonite.

Since the work has been progressing,
and the buildings quite complete,
We recognize it as a blessing,
where our aged members meet.

The surroundings to the highway,
spacious lawn, perfect and green;
The background, we would all say,
is as fine as can be seen.

The motive, we should mention,
before we do proceed,
is to give special attention
to those who stand in need.

A Home that has been granted
by our Father from on high,
where seed is sown and planted,
and a harvest by and by.

My sister and my brother
who shall occupy this place,
and the feeble homeless mother,
enjoy Heaven's richest grace.

May our walks through life implore
an elevated plane
And safely launch us on that shore
where heaven will be our gain.

(Author unknown)

The Rohrer Trio

A very energetic resident, Lloyd H. Rohrer, lived in the Home from 1958 to 1999. He with his sisters Vera and Miriam were siblings from the same family of Daniel Rohrer, who farmed and had an orchard near Manheim.

Lloyd was a friendly character and liked by most residents and employees. He was unique in his ways and could remember some riddles and jokes that he had heard from others. Then, due to being mentally challenged, he would tell these jokes to gain some recognition. Most folks around the Home gave him time to repeat his stories. He was usually very friendly and joyful with his work and relationships.

He worked well alongside maintenance personnel as he mowed grass, gathered trash, distributed newspapers, and bundled them for disposal after their use. He worked long days and usually put a lot of work into the hours he worked. It was a privilege to be able to give him and his sisters a home for many years.

Lloyd's conduct with others was usually above reproach. If perchance someone felt mistreated by him, the victim would say,

"Do you want me to tell Paul?" Usually people did not report him for the first such case since we needed to make allowance for his personality. Nevertheless, at times his desire for recognition would launch into overdrive. When his infractions became overwhelming, someone reported him to the Administrator. He really liked that because then he would have the opportunity for a session in the Administrator's office.

For Lloyd, that was a real ego trip, suggesting prestige and a high level of important business. His infractions usually came from a desire for more attention. Hence, he would come up behind an employee and "tap" them on the shoulder. The female employees were usually quick to report him, but the male employees could tolerate his "shoulder tapping" a bit easier. When his actions became overbearing, someone informed me, "It's time for you to see Lloyd again."

His trip to my office usually put a big smile on his face, giving a publicity message to those around him. The conversation in my office usually went something like this:

Administrator: Lloyd, why do you think you were asked to come into my office?

Lloyd: I don't know; I guess to talk a little.

A: Yes, that's true, but what should we talk about?

L: I guess whatever; but do you know what she did to me?

A: Who?

L: That employee; she made a face at me.

A: What did you do that brought you in here?

L: I just touched her on the shoulder with my hand.

A: Well, Lloyd, that is enough for you to be reported. The women employees do not like you doing that, so the rule is, No touching the female employees, or the male ones either. Try to think before you do such things.

L: Okay, Paul, I'll try to do better.

And he did do much better, sometimes for weeks at a time, but then he would falter, then a good talk in the office helped again.
Lloyd did seem to be well schooled on the issues of right and wrong, but he needed these sessions to remind him of his expected conduct.

Spiritually, I believe Lloyd knew right from wrong and knew the story of God's love through Jesus Christ as his Savior.

My friend, as you read these memoirs, it is my prayer that, if you do not know Jesus as your Savior and Lord, you would seek out a trusted friend to help you "walk to Jesus."

Lloyd's sisters, Miriam and Vera Rohrer, were also living in the Home.

A Master Teacher

Emily Kraybill lived to be ninety-seven years old, and thirteen of those years she lived at the Home. Born March 4, 1898, she came to live at the Home on May 10, 1982; she went to her heavenly home on March 8, 1995. Emily was a special person to the author because she was his schoolteacher for several years at the Willow Street Tin Shop, converted to a schoolhouse, and later at the New Danville Christian Day School. She expressed a warm Christian testimony of God's grace, and a sweet personality to all she met.

She also had a "firm" side of her personality, however, which she needed to manage a lively set of boys attending school under her as principal. She meant for rules to be obeyed and not broken. One day while the author was running through the school building to get away from those chasing him, Miss Emily was coming in through a door the same time the author was trying to exit the same opening. There was a collision of bodies, and the principal grabbed me by the arm in a firm grip and said, "Now, Paul, you know it is against the rules to run in this building. You must come by my office immediately." There were several others involved, but none of my buddies had smacked right into the principal. Each of the violators had to have their own session with Miss Emily.

So to the office I went, anticipating some severe discipline. After a good talk (hardly a scolding) from Emily, she laid out the activity for being so rude. The penalty was this: "Paul, I am requiring you to write five hundred times that 'I will not run through the schoolhouse again.'"

How long does it take to write that sentence on a yellow tablet? Well, it depends how the writer goes about it. We *nixnutz* (good-for-nothing) boys concocted a system to speed the process along. Taking four no. 2 lead pencils, we would wrap some masking tape around the pencils and go to work. We taped these pencils in a straight row alongside each other together and slanted the stack so that the points fit the line spacings on the tablet. Then, hurray, we were able to do four lines at a time to speed the process.

That part was acceptable, but the other part was not. We had to stay after school hours to do the job. Parents had to find out about our misconduct because the driver to take us home from school had to wait. Also, siblings are usually good storytellers, so there was no getting around some additional discipline after arriving home.

Miss Emily was a good elementary schoolteacher and a good disciplinarian. Teaching school was her lifetime career, influencing many children in a positive way as they learned the three R's, plus music, geography, and some Bible classes.

Soon after she moved into the Home, Emily came to my office to talk. I was happy to give her my utmost attention and all the time she needed to share what was on her heart. She said, "Paul, in the past I was over you as your teacher and you as my pupil. But now, you are over me as the Administrator, and I hope I will be as good a resident as you were a good pupil."

Emily was an excellent resident, an asset to the family of residents. She served on the Residents Council and was a helpful friend to anyone, wherever needed. I am sure she has received her crown of glory in the presence of her Savior and Lord.

A Faithful Dedicated Editor

Who could forget Elizabeth Bucher? Born October 17, 1900, she became a resident on December 21, 1970; she went to her eternal reward on April 1, 1994. On a daily basis she assured me of her prayers for me. Then with the usual twinkle in her eye, she would ask, "Paul, am I being a good girl in this wing where I live?" Paul assured her she was being a good girl and thanked her for being a fine resident. Elizabeth lived in a lovely suite facing Park City, on the second floor of the East Wing, as we called it in those days. The first floor was part of the Nursing Wing, for residents needing skilled care.

From 1972 through 1984, Elizabeth faithfully served as coeditor of *Highlights,* the Home's newsletter. The other coeditor, John R. Kraybill, terminated in 1984, but Elizabeth continued for three more years. After a total of fifteen years, with her health beginning to fail, she terminated and left the job of editing in the hands of a well-qualified editor, Mary Ella Herr.

Elizabeth had an interesting chuckle in her laugh, which always challenged her listeners to figure out what she was up to. She was a dear person, easygoing, and a devoted Christian. In her honor, the staff had a rose bed planted in the driveway island at the intersection of Harrisburg Pike and the Park City Loop Road. A plaque identifies this beautiful rose bed, for all passersby to read: "Given in honor of Elizabeth Bucher, for faithful volunteer service as editor to *Mennonite Home Highlights*, 1972 through 1984."

Longevity and Diligence

No resident or employee at the Home who had any interaction with Anna Snavely could forget her. I think her middle initial was H, since her mother's maiden name was Hershey. However, Anna's middle initial could well have been a W, which would have to stand for "Work" because that is really what she did most of the time as I knew her.

Anna was a single lady all her life, living at the Home from 1968. When she was sixteen months old, her mother died, so she was accepted into the home of Lizzie Heisey, near Manheim. She actually became like a birth sibling with Jonas Heisey, who was a son of Lizzie Heisey. Jonas also lived in the Home for his retirement years.

Anna gave many hours of service to the Home, which paid for her daily eight hours of work. But the time clock or a regular clock didn't stop Anna Snavely. No indeed! As I periodically walked through the facility, there was Anna working at some project, either in the kitchen, in the basement processing donated food, or helping the housekeepers or maybe the laundry girls. She had good rapport with employees and residents. Occasionally, however, she would have a run-in with Lloyd Rohrer; either they were arguing on some issue, or he was trying to tell her one of his silly jokes, which she didn't want to hear.

When asked how she liked living at the Home, she was quick to say, "Paul, I am well satisfied here since the day I moved in." My interview with her revealed that her life's work (and she did plenty of it) was cleaning for people in the community near where she lived. She also did gardening work for people. It was hard to find Anna sitting down and doing nothing at Mennonite Home. She had to be busy!

When I began employment there, the Home had a two-acre garden, producing a lot of food to be processed and stored for later use in residents' meals. Anna seemed to revel in doing what she liked to do and thereby felt fulfilled in life. When prompted for an interesting story, she said, "Paul, I'll tell you one! We had a strawberry patch here. In season, we picked the berries Monday, Wednesday, and Friday. There was this male resident who came here to live after he lost his wife. Now he was eager for companionship.

"For the whole season he helped pick strawberries each day we picked. But you know, Paul, he was a slow picker, or else he tried to be slow because I was a fast picker and would catch up to him. Then he would flirt with me about courtship. He wanted a woman in the worst way and tried to convince me to go out with him that very weekend. He made me so upset that I picked up my container of berries, walked straight into the building, set my berries down, and went to my room.

"Later, the head cook questioned me: 'Why did you quit picking berries so soon? Did you get sick or something?' I said 'no!' Then I told her, 'There just isn't enough room in the same berry patch for me and that flirting male resident. So that's that! Don't ask me to help pick berries anymore if he is picking at the same time.' That settled the attempted courting fling! Anna was not about to be hooked up with a man: she liked her independence and carried out that decision for her entire life.

Songwriter Resident

Edith Witmer was a remarkable woman. She was born October 28, 1902, as an only child of wealthy parents, Jacob and Mary (Brubaker) Witmer, of Donegal, near Mt. Joy, Pennsylvania. Edith became a resident at the Home on January 15, 1977, until her heavenly homegoing on June 19, 1982. She was a friendly woman and often stopped by my office to share her life's story and some of her unfulfilled dreams of life.

She became a songwriter when she penned the words to the song entitled "Teach Me Thy Truth." It is a well-known song among Mennonite congregations churchwide and appears in their hymnals. Many times a songwriter actually pens the words of their own personal theology, what they really believe. Thus, singing such songs helps Christians to commit their lives to God in "service," as thanks for all he has done for them personally.

After writing this hymn, she also wrote other articles about her pilgrimage with Jesus and had them published in the *Gospel Herald*, a churchwide periodical. Edith shared with the author comments she received from people who would remark to her, "If I could write a hymn like that, I would continue writing more." However, Edith commented, "It is not that easy, because hymns are 'born' and not 'made.' One does not pick up a pencil and write a hymn. Hymns come from the writer's own experience of living for the Master Teacher, living out the principles of the Word in everyday life. Famous writers like Charles Wesley and Fanny Crosby could do so, but certainly not me." Edith was modest in promoting what she could do because anything done well and worthwhile came via inspiration and a connection with her love for God and his Word.

The vision to write this hymn came to her while listening to the radio program entitled *A Hymn for Today!* While she was teaching at Goshen College, Goshen, Indiana, it had a motto for students to follow: "Culture for Service." With her Christian-living background, she interpreted that to mean "Christian Service." Thus, her mind formulated the words to the song she wrote.

Once Edith had the words written, she sent them to the music director at Goshen College. He composed the music to the words, which in her opinion fit quite well. Later, four young men used her newly written song for their Vesper Quartet. After graduating, they dispersed to the mission field in four different areas of the globe. When they returned some years later, they sang this hymn again. She rejoiced because "In service, Lord, for Thee" were the very words that brought conviction to their hearts in the first place, and a factor leading them to the mission field.

There was a time when she thought of the mission field call for herself, in a teaching position in South America. But the answer to her prayer always came back clearly: "You are not strong enough for the rigors of a foreign mission assignment." She did, however, find great fulfillment in a career of teaching at Goshen College for many years. To be sure, Edith fulfilled her call from her Lord to follow him. This is the essence of life, to step out in faith for God, following him daily, and to be of "service, Lord, to Thee!" Are you, dear reader, experiencing this joy of service? You really can by yielding your life to the Master Teacher of all time!

Chapter 21

Yearning for Independent Living Services

By the spring of 1982, I was meeting with a circle of other Administrator friends in the booming Mecca of retirement facilities in Lancaster County. I found that Mennonite Home was the only one not offering Independent Living accommodations. As a rather young Administrator, I developed the feeling that Mennonite Home was not quite fulfilling its purpose when compared to others in the surrounding locale. Was I an inefficient leader? Why couldn't we start building cottages to meet the requests of those on our waiting list?

My dream was to develop the land on the north side of the Harrisburg Pike since it was already designated for development, with a sewer and public water system installed. Sometime during the fall of 1982, the Administrator of the Home made an exploratory contact with the East Hempfield Township Manager, to determine what would be required to develop that tract of land.

One major requirement was to have a second egress onto the Harrisburg Pike from the Landis tract, which I hoped could become available to build on. As I saw it at the time, one could provide a second access by cutting a roadway from Harrisburg Pike, through the Raymond Adair property, and to the Landis tract. We envisioned this roadway to go into the prospective acreage just west of the existing bridge over the Little Conestoga Creek. This location would make it easy access for the Home's west-end driveway.

Over the next several winter months and on into spring, I would make periodic visits with Raymond Adair in his tobacco cellar, where he was usually busy stripping his tobacco crop. He was an interesting person to get to know. In his soft-spoken way, he would ask questions about the plans we had for the Landis tract. Then, as he listened to some more of my gabbing away about the Mennonite Home wanting to build Independent Living facilities, he would spew out of his mouth the longest stream of tobacco juice that I ever saw.

What an odor! I was surely glad not to be in the way when the stream of juice came out of his mouth. Without fail, after those days of visiting Raymond Adair in his tobacco cellar, my wife would sniff as I entered our house and say, "Wow, I can tell where you were today. Why don't you let me air out your suit, so it is fit to wear again?" So, off came the suit, and for several hours she had it hanging on the wash line outside to air out the tobacco smell. This usually worked temporarily, but eventually we had to have it thoroughly dry-cleaned to be acceptable.

After several days and weekly visits with him, he would ask, "What do you need from me to be able to build on the Landis land?"

In my eagerness to move forward with my ideas, I explained to him that we would need a second access to Harrisburg Pike in addition to the area of road frontage for access, just west of the house where Park and Betty Myers lived. Betty was a daughter of Raymond and Mary Adair.

"How do you intend to get the access you need?" he asked. "I do not have any land to sell."

I continued to explain that my idea was only to pay for a right of way through the flood-plain land down by the bridge.

"How would that look," he asked?

I suggested that our Land Planner and I could set a few stakes through that flood plain area, showing him how a driveway could take shape without infringing on any of his tillable land. He finally consented to have the stakes set across the flood plain to see how it would look.

Within a day or two, the Land Planner and I set about twenty-five stakes, showing a possible curved driveway from the Harrisburg Pike, through the flood plain, which would open up the possibility of developing the Landis land. But while we were placing the stakes, Mary Adair was watching intently from the porch. I wondered what she was thinking. I had not talked with any of the family to this point, only with Raymond in his tobacco cellar, and I thought he gave his consent.

I found out the hard way that "It is better to wait on God and trust him" than to move ahead without light from God. But, didn't I pray about the need for the right of way, and didn't Raymond Adair agree to have the stakes set? Well, I thought so! No doubt in my assertiveness and eagerness to move ahead, I missed the phrase where Paul says, "But if we hope for what we do not yet have, we wait for it patiently" (Romans 8:25).

The very next morning, soon after I was in my office, the receptionist let me know that someone was out front to see me. I went out, and sure enough, the two Adair sisters and a son-in-law wanted to talk with me. They had several stakes in their hands. I invited them into my office via the back porch door, and they readily agreed to come in that way. As I let them into the building, they told me in no uncertain terms that neither Mennonite Home nor anyone else would come through their property to build on the Landis farmland, and if I insist, a lawyer will be looking me straight in the eye and set things straight.

My intentions were good, but my procedure and timing was way off. In reflection, it would have been better to invite the whole family of daughters, their spouses, and the parents (Raymond and Mary Adair) to a luncheon and talk together about the needed proposal. At any rate, God worked it out in his own time, achieving a better plan than what I had first planned.

As I reflect on that experience twenty-three years ago, I knew then that I should heed the words of Scripture explicitly. The psalmist said, "Trust in the Lord and do good; . . . Delight yourself in the Lord and he will give you the desires of your heart. Commit your way to the Lord; trust in him and he will do this" (Psalm 37:3–5).

Dear reader, if the Lord is speaking to you about an area in life that needs to be changed or turned around, give yourself to trust him fully, and do so now. Life will be so much more fun to live with yourself, others, and above all with God the Almighty, who is Sovereign and wants to love you and give what is best for your life. I found this to be true. I learned some lessons the hard way, which you can perhaps avoid in your life. God is good!

The neat thing about that whole situation was for me to learn the lesson of waiting on God's timing. Just ten years later, after many hours of prayer and planning, the entire Adair family was eager to sell their parcel of land and buildings to Mennonite Home for the development of future phases of Woodcrest Villa. When they saw the beautiful buildings of Woodcrest Villa Phase I and the open-house ceremonies of Woodcrest Villa in 1993, they expressed kind words of congratulations for such a fine facility to care for the elderly.

Finally, Woodcrest Villa comes into being: Phase I opens November 1993, as happy new residents move into Robin Ridge, Meadow Lark, and Humming Bird Inn, where the dining room is located.

I was happy to be a part of the ceremonies experienced with the Adair family and the Board of Trustees, when the Home purchased 25.6 acres of land from the Adairs in the summer of 1994. Do you know what the Scripture has to say? "God is able to make all grace abound to you, so that in all things at all times, having all that you need, you will abound in every good work" (2 Corinthians 9:8). Indeed, God is good, and he will supply your every need through faith and trust in him.

Finally, after many hours of planning, borrowing many dollars for buildings, Mennonite Home, Inc., was able to offer comfortable living accommodations for seniors who wanted a maintenance-free lifestyle for their retirement years. When God is in it and we follow his timing, we always receive abundantly more than we can even ask for or think about, because God blesses those who put their faith and trust in him. Praise his wonderful name!

Chapter 22

Flying High and Having Fun!

Blessing Others in Retirement

Ann Garber Phillips was one (among many) of the sweetest born-again persons living at Mennonite Home. Born first on January 18, 1907, she became a resident on December 11, 1985; and went to meet her Maker on September 23, 1999. I was not able to find a date for her second birth (born again), but there were a multitude of evidences that proved she knew Jesus as Savior and Lord in her life.

Ann was the widow of a Methodist minister and for many years served the Lord alongside him. We talked together numerous times while she lived, circulated among staff, and made frequent visits to the office to have a chat. She was a delight to talk with! Her conversation would center on how good God is to her, and the ministry of service God had given her. She was an ardent prayer warrior for others and assured the author of her daily prayers for strength, wisdom, and patience for him as he carried the heavy responsibilities of administrating.

She was well-respected for her keen insight into the Scriptures and her ability to share her testimony with others. Ann was a giving and outgoing person. She did things to make others happy, and in so doing she herself experienced the "joy of the Lord" in her heart.

This lady owned an island (!) on the St. Lawrence River in Ontario, Canada, just over the border from the United States. The island is part of the Thousand Island chain and about two acres in size. It was big enough to have a nice three-bedroom cottage with a wide veranda around the front, and a big wooden deck on the backside of the house. The roof was painted bright red, and thus the name of her island was Red Top.

Access to the island was via a marina for small outboard motorboats, which she and her grandchildren used to travel from the mainland near Brookville, and across the water to Red Top. The boat trip took about a half hour, considering the time to undock from the marina and then dock at her island. She would go there to vacation for about three months each summer. Family would take her to the Canadian side at Brookville, Ontario, to her boat dock. It was a long drive and took most of one day to arrive and boat across the river.

Since the Administrator had his own Cessna 172 (a four-place aircraft) and a desire to see her island, he offered to fly her up one early summer, to take a weekend break. She was delighted to try this exciting adventure, to see how she would like it. The first trip went well, with good weather, a smooth ride, and lots of fun. It was even fun going across the river in her boat as she and her grandson navigated. Since I had an instrument license to fly if the weather was marginal or even requiring instrument flying, we usually made the trip according to her plans to go. Ann enjoyed this trip so well that she asked the Administrator to do the service each year, which required a trip to take her up to Ontario, and then in late August to fly there again to bring her back to Lancaster.

The location was ideal for a relaxing weekend out of the office, usually leaving Friday evening or Saturday (depending on the weather), and returning Sunday evening to be back to work on Monday. Her grandson and family would meet us at the Kingston, Ontario, airport. We would clear customs, drive to the dock, and navigate to the island. By the time we relaxed for an hour or so, Ann would have a scrumptious meal prepared for everyone. Erma and I had a great time with Ann and her grandson's family. We would visit, talk, stay overnight in one of the bedrooms, and fly back the next day. This was a usual routine for about five years as I provided this service for Ann.

On the two last trips we made, she would be weary and the plane ride was smooth, so Ann usually had about a two-hour nap while flying back to Lancaster. It was a real treat to know her and listen to her stories of ministry as she served the Methodist Church alongside her husband.

When I had purchased the 1979 Cessna 172 four-place aircraft, I wished to use it for travel to visit our son and his family in Indiana, and our other two sons living in Harrisonburg, Virginia. I was a private pilot from 1963 and at first could fly only when the weather was good. After several years, as I learned that this aircraft could be useful for necessary travel, I invested some more time and money to acquire an instrument rating and a commercial ticket. This enabled me to fly the aircraft for the good of others. In committing the investment to God, he enabled me not only to have fun flying, but also to transport others to places they desired to go.

As I reflect on some trips in the aircraft, I remember one trip to Louisville, Kentucky, for the Mennonite Health Association meeting. The Director of Nursing (DON), her husband, and an office person were making this eventful trip with me. We always prayed before firing up the aircraft engine, asking God for traveling mercies, his protection, safety, and good weather to and from the meeting. This travel in a private plane was much more economical than via the airlines, and it gave the pilot more hours of flying experience.

On this particular trip, the husband of the DON was up front in the seat beside me, to help navigate with the map, and also be on the lookout for other aircraft traffic. The weather was good but a bit breezy because a strong cold front had gone through the day before. This frontal passage provided some headwinds, making our travel speed a bit slower than desirable. One stop for fuel at a Morgantown, West Virginia, airport was eventful. The headwind was gusty, so when landing, the aircraft bounced once on the wheels and then settled down for the roll out to the taxiway. I'm sure my passengers were somewhat apprehensive about that landing.

The rest of the trip was routine, with a good landing at Louisville and inspiring messages and fellowship at the meeting. However, the DON and her husband decided to find another way back to Lancaster, by car with other friends. Perhaps their trust in this Administrator-pilot was wavering a trifle. So the other lone office person and I as pilot flew the whole way back to Lancaster, with one stop for fuel. We had a good tailwind for speed and good landings because the wind had become calmer, and by now the pilot had more experience. It is always good to pray, asking the Lord for guidance, protection, and safety in all travel, which is a good way to honor him in life.

There were additional trips for the Mennonite Health Association meetings, with some Home personnel to Boston; to Penn State, Pennsylvania; Orlando, Florida, and numerous other places around the country. Our flight level usually was anywhere from six to eight thousand feet, depending on headwinds or tailwinds and the weather en route. I loved to fly, acquiring nearly 2,500 hours of flying experience over a period of about twenty-five years of flying besides working at a full-time job. I praise the Lord for his protection and safety for all that flying.

One time while coming back to Lancaster from Virginia, there were heavy, thick clouds most of the way and thunderstorms spotted around in a wide area. I prayed, asking the Lord for safety and a good flight. The National Flight Service Station gave me a report of instrument flying weather and a compass heading that would keep me out of any thunderstorm activity. As we climbed out to altitude, the controller directed me to fly a seventy-degree heading to stay clear of thunderstorms.

The Lord provided a clear area for us to fly, with thunderstorms all around to the right and the left of our travel heading, but not a storm in our path of flight. How good God is! It reminded me of the time Moses stood at the bank of the Red Sea, and God divided the waters on the right and the left, making a path of dry land for the Israelites to pass over to the other side. What a miracle! We serve a wonderful God, who looks out for his children in times of need.

Chapter 23

Interesting Tidbits: Residents and Employees

The Residents Council provided some interesting comments that are worthy of note. Most of the comments were handwritten and put in the suggestion box, for the council's president to read at the monthly meetings. In my role as Administrator, the residents expected me to attend the monthly meetings, or to have a representative attend if I could not come. The following candid comments reflect what residents were thinking about the Home's operation:

1. Such a good spaghetti dinner and bread sticks. It was like eating at Olive Garden.

2. The number of new employees disturbs me; are they replacing, or adding new?

3. Mr. Leaman read our rights to us, and then took them away because we can't walk across Harrisburg Pike to Weis Market to get candy or stop at the concrete median island until traffic is past.

4. While I'm complaining, I wonder how visitors are impressed with some casual dress on Fridays. A certified nursing assistant (CAN), wearing faded blue-denim farmer's bib overalls, wheeled a lovely, refined lady in a wheelchair to the chapel for a viewing. Is there no respect for anybody?

5. We as residents are complaining about our clothing not coming back to the proper residents. This is happening regularly when residents send their clothing to the laundry without identifying marks. This place needs a new government that can do something about the crooks in the laundry.

6. I think it is terrible. Some people want to be such good

Christians, but they leave the breakfast table before Bible reading and prayer.

7. Since the Home has grown, would we as residents be willing to designate money to the Endowment Fund to help the poor rather than lavishly decorating the place for the upcoming Christmas season?

8. I didn't think you Mennonites would have lady preachers. And furthermore, why do women give devotions in the dining room over the public speaker system? The Bible says no!

9. Did you know this particular resident's personality has changed? He has threatened that old Mr. Leaman for his life, and others too.

10. In behalf of the family, we thank the Home personnel for their faithful care and support of her during the six years she lived here, and the benevolent fund for helping when her money ran out. May God bless you all!

11. [Overheard at breakfast:] There was only one Friday the 13th in the year 1960, and it came on May 7th.

12. [Heard in a hall or at breakfast:] How many seconds are in a year? (Only 12: January 2nd, February 2nd, etc., making a total of 12 seconds for the year!)

13. [Dr. Harry Hoffman took his work as Medical Director very seriously. Overheard in conversation with the Home's Matron:]

Doctor, did you call me yesterday?

Why no. Why do you ask?

Well, I passed here yesterday and saw a hearse or dead wagon out front. Who died?

Why, no one that I am aware of. What you saw was the Rawleigh man trying to sell some remedies for the residents.

14. [From an alert staff person:] Last week we had a man who thought he was sick enough to have a food tray brought to his room for breakfast, but he was good enough to walk down the stairs and all the way to the nurses station to tell them he wanted his toast bread toasted light. Now that really takes the cake!

15. The ultimate test of an institution is not in its financial solvency, its accreditation, or its popular acclaim, but rather, Do its residents have hope?

16. [The Food Service Director came in a bit late after a seminar on "Respect for Personal Image" and met the Administrator in the hall:]

Paul, I'm sorry to be late, but I just discovered in our seminar yesterday why it takes ladies so much longer to get dressed.

Why is that?

We women have to slow down for all the curves as we dress.

17. [One Friday afternoon the same Food Service Director met the Administrator in the hall as she was leaving for the weekend:]

Paul, do you know how far it is from one of your ears to the other?

No, not really. But what's the joke?

[While moving her hand and fingers walking up the side of her head, from the left ear to the right:] Why, Paul, don't you see? It's a trip over the week/weak end!

18. [A longtime employee, serving as an LPN:] One morning I got awake, and it was way past my time to be at work. I couldn't believe it. Was I getting so forgetful? So I quickly called the Home to tell them I'm coming but will be a little late, only to be told that it was not my day to work.

19. Then there were difficult administrative duties that I had to do. I remember when the Charge Nurse and the Personnel Director had to admonish an employee who was not performing to expected criteria. The employee had received numerous warnings about her conduct, and even some coaching on how to improve performance, but to no avail. To bring closure to the situation, they had to send her to the Administrator's office.

After hearing her side of the story and the Nursing Supervisor's findings, the Administrator had to make the final determination. My decision came after prayer for guidance each day before coming to work: "There is the door. We believe it is for your best interest to use your abilities elsewhere, perhaps in some other line of employment." In certain times past, such a tense situation would have caused me to become rather dictatorial. But the Holy Spirit flooded my mind with a calmness of spirit in my tone of voice and body language to handle the issue professionally. Praise the Lord for his goodness!

Anyone listening in the hallway would have heard the following: "You can't do that to me. I have two children to support. I need the money."

The Administrator said in a calm and compassionate tone of voice, "I'm sorry, but there is the door. That's my answer."

After more vehement words, and a few cusswords thrown in for emphasis by the employee, she added, "But. Paul, I am going through a divorce. I won't have any job or money. I am going to see a lawyer. You can't do this to me."

"There is the door" was the calm reply. Sadly, it had to happen for the sake of the residents. These kinds of tasks were never easy. There were only a few such workers; nevertheless, these situations always caused my stomach to churn the wrong way. As I reflect on that experience, my only regret is that I did not take the time to pray with the employee, asking God to help her find a job compatible with her expertise, and to leave the door of opportunity open for her to find a relationship with her Maker.

20. To keep in touch with residents, employees, and visitors, I would sometimes eat a Sunday noon meal in the dining room, especially when I was responsible to bring the message for the residents in the chapel. On this particular Sunday, we enjoyed a really tasty meal, including delicious vanilla pie with crumbs on top. Several visitors were also eating there that Sunday. I knew one couple fairly well and realized that he could be a good jokester at times. He sat just two tables from me across the dining room. While eating his pie, he called over, "Paul, this pie is musty. Should I finish it?"

I was eating my piece of the same pie, and mine tasted "musty" too. But I went ahead and ate it anyway. Remembering this friend's jokes, I replied, "Yes, John [not his real name], you may go ahead and have your second piece." It was so good that I was contemplating my second piece, too! Since he liked the pie so much, he decided that he "must" have another piece, and he did so!

However, this little episode was too good to let go by. On Monday morning, when the (fairly new) Food Service Director arrived on duty, I went to the kitchen and asked her if I could see her for a few minutes in my office. She readily came, not imagining what could be wrong so early on a Monday morning. I addressed her by her first name and said, "Yesterday I was here for dinner, as well as some good friends of mine. When we got to the dessert, this friend of mine told me his piece of pie was 'musty.'"

"Did you have pie, Paul?" she asked.

"Yes, I did!"

"Was yours musty too?"

"Well, as a matter of fact, it was."

"What did you and your friend do about it?"

"Well, I went ahead and ate mine, and he did too, as well as all those at his table. But I think about all the others in the dining room who didn't say anything at all about it. I guess it might come up in Residents Council this week if it was bad enough."

"Oh, Paul, it couldn't have been musty. They were freshly delivered on Friday, frozen solid, and then baked late Saturday afternoon or evening, so they had to be fresh." She had a worried look on her face. "I'll look into it immediately."

By this time I could hardly keep from laughing and was almost feeling guilty for pulling a good joke on this fine lady, recently hired as Food Service Director. She saw the growing look of mischief on my face and said, "Paul, are you pulling a joke on me?"

"Why, of course I am. What would the workplace be like if we couldn't have a little fun or a good laugh sometimes? With pie so good, we 'must' have a second piece, which my friend did and so did I."

After we both had a good laugh, I affirmed her for the great work she was doing in her new job, and she thanked me for the compliments received. However, it was a learning experience for both of us, getting to know how we function under various situations. Needless to say, she was prepared the next time I was eager to tell her about a situation relating to the Dietary Department.

21. I heard a story on how the elderly in bygone years celebrated fifty years of marriage. This particular couple was married before automobiles, so any distance they wanted to travel was by train. Their honeymoon was a trip by train to a distant city, where they had a reservation in a hotel for a one-night stay. The next day they would take the train back to their hometown. That was the extent of their honeymoon since they were short of money and couldn't afford any more.

Each year as their anniversary came around, they took the same trip away and home again, doing this for forty-nine years. On their fiftieth anniversary, not wanting to break tradition, they took the same trip, to the same city, and stayed in the same hotel for their celebration. However, the next morning, planning to take the same train trip back home for the fiftieth time, they missed the train. So, for the first time in fifty years, they had to stay in the same hotel the second night. This irked the husband deep inside because he wanted to do some odd jobs around their place the next day, but he didn't say anything to his wife, not wanting to upset her feelings.

As they were preparing for bed that night, she said to her husband, "Isn't this wonderful? We get to stay the second night in this lovely hotel? Why, I am feeling absolutely romantic, Honey. Won't you join me in bed soon? I just feel like I have Summer in my heart and am warming up, Fall in my spirit for falling in love again, and [as she left her hair down] Winter in my hair. Won't you join me?"

"Well yes," he replied, "but you know, Dear, if you would have had Spring in your feet, we would not have missed the train!"

There were many more interesting tidbits that happened or were voiced by longtime employees, which helped make this new job exciting and interesting. At times I had to be on my guard. After several night-shift visits with the nurses to experience their type of work at night, one longtime nurse aide made a quick comment from her perspective, sharing what she thought of me as the new Administrator: "Boy, do you ever make a good impression, Paul. Anytime you wish, you can park your shoes under my bed." What was she saying? That is one temptation I didn't want to dwell on.

S.H., CNA gave this testimony about her relationship with a resident: "I lost my brother in the Navy, . . . it was hard to come back to work after the funeral. I was very close to E. Miller, who couldn't talk much anymore. I went to her for comfort, . . . the first thing I noticed was she was wearing a blue and white striped outfit like the Navy wore. I hugged her, told her I loved her, and she was able to say "I love," and the whole day was brighter for me after that."

Another experience from S.H. "Every year we took residents to Cherry Hill Orchards, . . . and there was this man Mr. Bender, a retired farmer. He would climb right up into the tree, picking many cherries as he climbed. Every time the bucket was full, we had to retrieve the bucket from him, pour the cherries into a bag to be weighed, . . . he became enraged because I was taking his cherries away. When I cam back, he had his shoes off, and was stuffing his shoes with cherries to hide them, because he didn't like me taking the cherries that he picked.

L.F., LPN, a single person, so to build friendships with residents, she would often invite those who could, to come to her house for a meal. One particular resident really cherished the hospitality of a fellow resident who always had a smile for everyone. She was a faithful prayer warrior for the Administrator, staff, and other residents. Even though she had a meager supply of funds, she would always find a $5.00 bill to contribute to a needy cause to be used where needed most. L.F. LPN would agree, "these kind of experiences made it all worthwhile to work in nursing care for the joy of interaction with the residents." She also shared about the good rapport she had with Charlotte Yoder, then Administrator of Health Services, and said, "Paul what is her role at Woodcrest Villa? I really admire and am really amazed how Charlotte climbed up the ladder in the organization. I'm really glad for her."

Chapter 24

Personal Encounters with Residents

Serving as a minister for twenty-three years and in several congregations before taking the job at Mennonite Home, the residents occasionally requested that I preach for their Sunday morning worship time. This particular Sunday morning, I shared on the subject of being a servant: First, serving God in response for what he has done for us through his Son, Jesus Christ. Second, serving each other for the good of all, through daily contacts with the surrounding community. Third, serving those under our care in this facility.

I emphasized the importance of each person and that the jobs are of equal value even though we recognize the level of responsibility each position requires. The Administrator is no better or of more importance than an employee who does housekeeping chores or other jobs in each department. The difference is the level of responsibility each employee has in their assignment.

My theory was really tested after the service that Sunday. As the residents were walking out of the assembly, I was greeting each with a handshake, wishing them God's best in their lives. Soon there was a strong and poignant odor permeating the whole atmosphere. I looked in the direction where some residents were already sidestepping the feces that were dropping on the floor each step the ninety-year-old resident was taking. He had a serious mishap. Since it was a Sunday morning, only a skeleton housekeeping crew was on duty, and none in the area where we had the service. Wow! What a sight to behold, and the odor was almost unbearable.

What should be done and by whom? I quickly left off shaking hands, went to the janitor's closet, and got a mop, warm water, and detergent. I asked the residents to clear the area. They rapidly complied, but some stood by, observing this Administrator mopping up the floor while wearing a white shirt, tie, and good suit. One elderly lady resident came by and said, "Well, Paul, today you had to practice what you just preached, didn't you?"

Another interesting comment about a "poop" story. One particular, and interesting employee was the front receptionist to greet people who came to the facility. Occasionally, she would need to accept small packages delivered by UPS. These packages would invariable be packed with the very light fluffy white odd shaped Styrofoam packing material to protect the items inside. On this particular day, the receptionist was asked to open the package. She did, and upon doing so, this fluffy white packing went flying all over the floor of the front office. What a sight for any visitor or another employee to behold. In fact, the receptionist was even somewhat embarrassed, however, she took life in stride, often making an interesting remark about an embarrassing episode. So, the receptionist quickly began to try and gather the wayward Styrofoam white fluffy material into a pile and retrieve it. The more she tried, the further the white fluffy material scattered. When asked what she was doing by her supervisory she replied, "Oh, I'm trying to clean up this 'angel poop' off the floor." What an interesting comment! We who had gathered around the incident had a hearty laugh over the episode, and her sense of humor.

One Thursday evening the supervisor was handing out the paychecks to the staff on duty. This was before direct deposit. The supervisor arrived in Rosevue II stating, "Paychecks are here." "I didn't get a paycheck." The supervisor responded, "Well Millie, you need to clean up the poop." Millie looked the supervisor directly in the eyes, stopped shaking and said, "I didn't clean up the poop. It's not my job." The supervisor responded, "Well Millie, that is why you didn't get a paycheck."

Another interesting encounter: "A 90 year old Mennonite lady came to Mennonite Home with her head in a halo brace due to a fractured neck. This brace is a metal frame that keeps her head and neck straight while the broken neck heals. She was sitting in her room holding the newspaper up so she could read it. A confused resident wandered into her room and switched the light off. Fannie sweetly responded to the resident calling her by name saying she needed the light on to read. The confused resident responded, 'Who do you think is paying the electric bill around here anyway?' Staff informed the supervisor of the incident, so the supervisor went into the resident's room and said, "What is this I hear about you running up the electric bill?" This was funny to the newspaper reader, and she just laughed and laughed until the tears came."

Nurses experience life as well as death in caring for residents. One evening a very elderly lady was dying and her two children were around her bed singing to her. At 11:00 P.M., they were singing the song, "Stepping on shore and breathing new air." Just at that moment the woman took a deep breath, stopped breathing here on earth but really did breathe in the 'new heavenly air' of her final home." What a beautiful way to depart this world. Friends, have you made that all important decision to accept Jesus Christ into your life, and be assured that at the end, you will be with your Savior Jesus Christ occupying one of the mansions prepared for you? John 14:1-6 (NIV)

Money, Money, Everywhere

One rather mild spring day, the Emergency Equipment sirens were blaring, and many residents went out on the front porch to see what was happening! There was a bank robbery at one of the branch banks at Park City Mall. The next day, the Lancaster paper's front page had a descriptive write-up about the robbery. One rather thin elderly resident—clothed with baggy blue-denim bib overalls and having a dry sense of humor and little financial resources—was reading the article by the front desk outside my office door. Since he was somewhat a loner in personality type, I asked him, "How are you doing today?"

"I was reading this article about the bank robbery," he said. "I was just wondering how they did that?"

He didn't really want to try it, did he? Upon hearing his remark, I certainly hoped he was only thinking out loud and not really planning any action on how to acquire funds for his scant supply.

Several months after the Park City Bank robbery, there was another exciting episode just across the street from the Home, and a few yards into the Park City Loop road. A Brinks Security truck was traveling west on Harrisburg Pike, and while turning right onto the Park City Loop road, the back door of the truck flew open. Apparently it was not properly latched. Out rolled several muslin bags of coins the truck was transporting to a local bank. As the bags hit the pavement, they burst open on impact, spilling coins all over the roadway.

Coins were rolling in all directions. Motorists stopped to help or perhaps to grab some quick cash, and someone called 911. Police soon arrived on the scene and closed the Loop road to all traffic, so the helping motorists soon cleared out. The sirens of the police and a fire truck really stirred the interest of our residents. Perhaps some low-income ones would have liked to keep all the coins they could gather in fifteen minutes, but that did not become an option.

The Fire Department personnel soon had the coins swept together in piles and shoveled them into new bags for the Brinks truck personnel. What an embarrassing episode! I wonder if someone received a pink slip for not latching the door on the Brinks truck. Uniformed police officers were walking around all over the street, retrieving coins that rolled way out to the fringes of the accident scene and had to be picked up by hand. Life is interesting, and such experiences in life call us to evaluate our faithfulness in the small and the larger responsibilities in our jobs, for the honor and glory of God.

Embarrassing and Humorous Experiences

After serving at the Home for about eighteen months, an elderly single lady asked me to visit her room. She called down to the receptionist-secretary and asked if she could have an interview with Mr. Leaman about some of the Home's policies. In those days, the Home was still a small operation and not yet able to afford a social worker, so I would try to accommodate such requests in my busy schedule. The appointment was set for 9:00 a.m. the next morning in the resident's room, on second floor of the building's old part.

At the appointed hour the next morning, I went to the resident's room, knocked on the door first (my consistent practice), and heard a cheery voice: "Come in!" I opened the door and walked in, expecting to resolve the issues on her mind. But was I ever embarrassed! Here she was, smiling broadly, sitting in her lounge chair and wearing only panties and a bra.

How would you (the reader) handle this situation? What issues did she want to talk about, anyway? Well, I didn't know exactly where to look, so I tried to concentrate on her face and look her in the eyes. However, I couldn't help but notice her petite bodily frame, with her navel clearly visible, and indeed, at her age of nearly eighty-five, someone could have said her skin texture needed ironing.

I was there to hear the issues at hand on her mind, so I suggested that she needed more time to finish dressing. But she said, "No, I'm dressed. I can handle it if you can."

"Well, is it alright if I come back later?" She reluctantly agreed. I politely suggested that I would return in thirty minutes and left. Thirty minutes later I returned, knocked, and heard the same cheery voice: "Come in!" I opened the door and walked in. She actually had dressed according to her standards, which was only the addition of a half slip added to her appearance. This elderly lady's idea of being dressed was different from mine, so I proceeded to look her in the eyes, communicate with her on the issues that were troubling her. We arrived at several solutions that she and I could both live with, and I was promptly on my way, thinking, *Wow, what am I getting into in this new job?*

Another resident's eyesight was getting worse by the year. Another resident told her, "If you drink plenty of carrot juice, it will heal your eyes and keep you from getting cancer or going blind." She went out to the grocery store, bought lots of carrots, took ownership of a corner of the basement, ground the carrots into pulp, squeezed the juice from the pulp, and drank it. She drank so much orange carrot juice on a regular basis that her skin turned orange.

Phares Kemrer told a story that came from Ella Herr, a sister to Bertha, wife of Phares. Ella's husband, Frank Herr, had a neighbor who cut down some cherry trees and sawed the logs into boards. One day when Frank visited him, his friend was nailing these beautiful cherry boards to make a calf pen near his barn. Since nice cherry lumber is expensive, Frank criticized his friend for using such good lumber that way. He convinced the farmer to sell him a pile of the lumber. Frank took it to his woodworking shop and built a nice cabinet for a grandfather clock works. Ella cherished that beautiful chiming clock as a gracious gift from her husband, Frank. It was in their living room till she passed on to her heavenly home.

Also, Phares told of a resident who asked him for some charcoal from the furnace room. He graciously gave her some, only to learn later that she used it to rub the chalky substance through her hair periodically, to keep it black. She did not like the idea of looking old, with white hair like the other elderly people. To her dismay, however, it all washed out when she washed her hair, streaking her face and body with a smudgy mess of black and fine coal dust, like soot. She soon quit using that way of coloring her hair.

An anonymous family member of a resident reported: "Grandma liked to eat shredded wheat for breakfast! She had a habit of chewing in her sleep. She chews on Grandpa's whiskers and thinks they're shredded wheat!"

In the early days of my administration, while the old buildings were still standing, the south wing had long balconies on each floor. There residents could sit on rocking chairs or hang their personal underclothing out to dry after it was hand-washed. From the south looking northward, one could see the corsets, petticoats, pantaloons, and other intimate underwear such as bras, if indeed they were worn in those days. What a sight! The top floor was for men only; women occupied the first and second floors.

One day a ninety-year-old male resident walked off the premises. The staff was not too concerned since others had done this several times and always came back. But this man did not return. I went looking for him, along with several nurses, but could not find him.

A motorist eventually found him walking along the road, stopped, and asked him for his wallet, to identify him. He knew enough not to hand his wallet to a stranger, became somewhat belligerent, and would not cooperate. The motorist did convince him to get into his car; the rambling resident was likely out of breath from walking so far. The driver took him to the Millersville Children's Home, thinking he belonged there. We later brought him back to his room without any further problems.

One resident (V. K.) shared an episode shared about another resident. As she walked into the room, the lady resident was huddled up, as though trying to keep warm. "Are you cold?" the visitor asked.

"Oh no. I just can't wait till I can go home, to my heavenly home."

Then her husband piped up: "What about me?"

"Oh, you'll just have to wait another five years," she replied, "because you are that much younger than me."

How's that for planning your demise? May this be a reminder that we need to be ready at all times, because we do not know when that day will be. Reader, are you ready to meet Jesus, if he should come today to take you to your eternal home? While working at Mennonite Home, I heard a saying: "The young may die, but the older persons must die." So be ready!

Motivating Others

Human Resources posted this statement on the employees bulletin board near the time clock:

How to Motivate the Unmotivated!
Important Notice! The management regrets that it has come to their attention that employees dying on the job are failing to fall down. This practice must stop, as it becomes impossible to distinguish between death and natural movement of the staff. Any employee found dead in an upright position will be dropped from the payroll.

A new slogan floated around Mennonite Home during the 1990s, triggered by an event among management staff during my Administration. Nelson Kling (current President at Mennonite Home) and I were in the East Hempfield Township Office, discussing issues for approval of the Woodcrest Villa project, along with a representative from the Land Planning firm. There was some controversy between the Township Manager and Land Planning personnel.

I was then CEO and eager to see the project get past many delays and move ahead. After too much controversy, a "light from heaven" seemed to switch on in my mind. I believe the Lord gave me an apt phrase: "Let's just do it!" The Township Manager quickly picked up on the slogan, liked it, and approved what we wanted, but not to the satisfaction of the Land Planning personnel. That was OK since Mennonite Home was paying the bill and in the driver's seat, so to speak.

Nelson and I liked the slogan so well that since then we used it many times as we worked together in management and launched other ideas among the staff. It is a good slogan. After generous time for input and discussion, a team eventually has to take action. The slogan speaks of the effort needed so urgently in managing any size of staff and projects and in generating teamwork.

Chapter 25

Words of Appreciation Shared

What would life be like if we lived each day, worked hard for long days, and never received a kind word or a special card that expresses appreciation from the sender to the receiver? Life could become dull, meaningless, and humdrum. But not at Mennonite Home! Many times employees went beyond the call of duty, sacrificing their time, giving of their love and care for those who carried a heavy load of work, stress, and at times frustration.

Following are excerpts from cards and handwritten notes, from residents, their families, and employees. They all helped to make my job, and the memories I have of working there, so interesting, enjoyable, and fulfilling. The first one is a card for Father's Day from my loving wife, Erma!

> Honey—It's your day. . . . Enjoy it—all the way!
> Hope this is a very special day. You're a great guy!
> I love the fun you bring into my life.
> You're the only one of a kind. I love you!
> - *Erma*

> We are so fortunate to have you as our leader, and I am thankful that God has blessed my life with your influence. Please know it makes me happy!
> - *Linda*

> All the personnel of Rosevue Nursing have gone beyond the call of duty, giving unconditional love to

Catherine, our sister, the three months she lived there. May God bless each one of you! —The Mowrer Family
Thank you again for your help in getting L. Wilson in the facility for nursing care. The care was superb! God works in mysterious ways, and this experience proved that to be true again! God bless you!
    - *M. Kline*

Dear Paul and friends of Mennonite Home:
How thoughtful you are to remember Peter with such a beautiful basket planter, and the inspiring card. He respects the individuals he worked with, and the entire organization!
    - *Anita Rohrer*

[Peter was the Accountant before his fall, resulting in a head injury that prevented him from continuing to work.]

Thank you again for the memorable and delightful time I had today on that surprise plane ride. The color of the leaves was so beautiful, giving me a greater appreciation for the creation!
    - *G. Hurst*

Accept our deepest thanks and appreciation for the loving, faithful, and tender care the staff gave in Rosevue and in Oakvue during the two years mother lived there. Your tender loving care provided us as family many precious memories we will not forget.
    - *The B. Ackerman family*

Thanks, Paul, for your part and others in paying half of the cost of M. Kreider's hearing aid.
    - *With love, A. Mary Kreider*

Thank you, Paul, for the opportunity to work at MH/WCV. I have many fond memories to take with me.
- J. Landis

Thanks so much for arranging us to come for a tour of WCV, and for a very delicious meal. I was highly impressed by the facilities. Obviously, you have done well to be in charge of a facility with such growth in a short time.
- N. Ressler

Dear Friends: Thanks for the flowers, the bag of goodies, and our new home in WCV. It is just wonderful!
- H. and C. Keller

This is a sincere (belated) thank-you note in appreciation for the Christmas bonus, and the fifteen-year employment gift. May God bless you as you work together to make MH a wonderful place to live and work!
- P. Good

Dear Paul, Nelson, and all the staff! I want to convey my thanks to all of you for the wonderful caring people you are. We both enjoyed living at WCV and learning to know so many wonderful friends.
- A. Dixon

Your kindness meant so much! On behalf of the 11:00 p.m. to 7:00 a.m. shift, we thank you for the delicious Easter dinner provided for us, and for Yvonne serving it to us in the employee dining room.
- *Gratefully, C. Walls, RN, and E. Stone, RN*

My family and I are extremely grateful for the kind loving care your nursing staff gave my father. At no time did we see anything but the highest quality of care. It

meant more than we can express to know he was in such good hands!
- *E. Charles & W. Good*

We would like to sincerely thank everyone involved with providing an environment of Christian care and love for our mother the past several years. Our family appreciated the use of the chapel for viewing purposes.
- *Sensenig Family*

Thank you, Paul, for coming to my drop-in (open house). It was a complete surprise to receive the plaque for my years of service. It was a wonderful experience working at MH.
- *V. Keener*

Tales Told about This Administrator

End-of-day frustration

Several weeks ago an Administrator sitting in his home decided to make a phone call to a friend. He dialed the number and heard a busy signal. After waiting for a time, he tried again, with the same result. *How can that line be busy all that time?* he thought. After waiting still longer, he dialed for the third time, feeling confident that he would get a clear line. But, alas again, he heard a busy signal. Suddenly he realized his problem: all the while he was dialing his *own* telephone number.

Paul was holding up his playing partners and having a terrible time getting around the golf course. "I'd move heaven and earth if I could just break a 100," he said to one of his golfing buddies.

"Concentrate on heaven," his buddy replied. "You've already moved plenty of earth [in the Home's building programs]."

Did you ever notice that when you reach a certain age, everything you have seems to wear out, spread out, or fall out?

While a family was having their Christmas party one weekend in the Parkvue Multi-purpose room, a youngster saw one of the little red boxes on the wall sporting the message, "Pull down lever." He did so, and off went the fire alarm buzzers, louder than he ever heard. Within minutes, firefighters were storming through the building, looking for the fire. It came to light that the author's young nephew had pulled the fire alarm. The firefighters knew the administrator and later kidded him about not having the control of group conduct.

Sometimes the food service department complained about how messy a group left a kitchenette after a weekend party. To improve the situation, the administrator found a motto and posted it in all the kitchenettes. Ten Golden Rules to Observe for Groups Using Parkvue, Meadowue, and Rosevue Activity Rooms:

If it spills Wipe it up!

If it falls Pick it up!

If it is taken out Put it back!

If it is yours Claim it!

If it cries Feed it!

If it breaks Replace it!

If it gets too hot Cool it!

If it is opened Close it!

If it is turned on Turn it off!

It is isn't understood how it works Leave it alone!

As time went on, people left the activity rooms in better condition, but obviously not everyone took the motto seriously. This convenience was a bonus to residents' families by the use of the rooms at no charge, so it was imperative that the facility be taken care of, and most families did a wonderful job. Many gave a contribution for the use of the rooms, while others expressed their thanks with a card.

Some heard this story from the author, speaking at a banquet in Bird-in-Hand about growing up in a small church in Lancaster County:

"We didn't have much money, but my mother could handle any situation. She always invited the preacher to dinner after church on Sunday, and he always gave excuses and never came. But one Sunday we were just sitting down to eat when we looked out the window and saw the preacher and his wife coming up the walk. There was one piece of chicken for each of us, and that was it. So Mom said, 'When the chicken is passed, you two oldest boys don't take a piece.' My older brother and I obeyed, and there was enough chicken. But when my sister brought in the pie for dessert, I knew we were in trouble. It was cut into just enough pieces for the family without the two visitors. But my mother remembered and said: "Now you two boys who didn't eat your chicken—no pie for you!"

A Few Riddles!

Some people are tall and don't fit in a bed;
others are small and still way ahead.
Hope this *big* box doesn't scare you out of your wits.
The one who packed it, almost had a few fits!

Open it up and you will see,
in fact, you might even be filled with glee.
It will give you a lift for the new year,
so use it as needed and have no fear!
—What am I?

There are times when you have to sit at quite a high angle,
In fact, it is then when your legs begin to dangle!
I have come to help you reach the things you couldn't, you see.
And to give you a lift to get where you wouldn't without me.
I hope you will like me, sit on me, step on me, kick me,
shove me, do what you like.
I'll still keep my shape, stand by you, support you, hold you,
without a bit of dislike!
—Who/what am I?

What Is My Name?

I have no respect for justice. I maim without killing. I break hearts and ruin lives. I am cunning and malicious, and gather strength with age. The more I am quoted, the more I am believed. I flourish at every level of society. My victims are helpless. They cannot protect themselves against me, because I have no name and no face. To track me down is impossible. The harder you try, the more elusive I become. I am nobody's friend. Once I tarnish a reputation, it is never the same. I topple governments and wreck marriages. I make innocent people cry in their pillows. My name is _____ .

Gems of the Day

"If the world seems like a cold place to you, toss a few logs on the fire and warm it up!"

"If life hands you a lemon, make lemonade, and share it with anyone."

From a card given by my very efficient secretary on Boss's Day: "Dear Boss: If the Secretary of Labor should come to the office to proclaim you as the Best Boss of the Year, remember one thing . . . : try to act surprised!" Footnote: "And if you're not here, I'll act surprised! —Joyce Turner Brunk

Conclusion to My Story and Reflections

Would I do it again? Yes! As I reflect on service, I realize that God has been very good to us as a family. In our lifetime of service, it was a wonderful experience to see how God worked

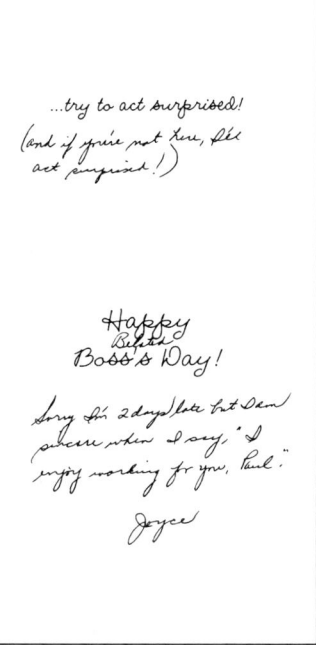

How to deal with the "powers that be"—with success!

out his way and will for our lives. As you have read, not all of life is beautiful roses. From time to time, life tries us and tests our faith and obedience to his divine plan. As you contemplate where your life is going, take courage! Give your life plans wholly to God, who knows all things, loves you, and wants the best for you in life!

I offer my sincere thanks to all of you who read this story and have had a part in the success and growth of Mennonite Home, as a resident, an employee, or part of the supporting and involved community. I pray that this story of reflections on my years of growing up, and then serving the Mennonite Home organization for twenty-one years, will be a blessing to your life personally and a glory to God. The Lord was a steadying guide even through mistakes and through successes enjoyed because of your part during these years.

My experiences of having fun during these twenty-one years were possible because of your dedication in service at Mennonite Home. I rejoice also in realizing that you extended your efforts in service to God, whether at work or in your personal life. As I reflect on the past accomplishments, it all happened because of the concerted efforts, dedication, and expertise of the Board of Trustees, the employees, the residents, their families, and the general public who together supported the ministry in healthcare.

"To God be the glory, great things He has done!" (Fanny Crosby).

—*Paul G. Leaman, NHA, RHP, M.Div.*

The Author

Paul G. Leaman grew up in Lancaster County, Pennsylvania, and worked on the 120-acre family farm until he was 23 years old. Then with his wife, Erma, he moved to the southern end of the county and for 13 years pastored a church across the state line, near Conowingo, Maryland, while earning his living through carpentry. Paul and Erma also served the Lord's mission in Atmore, Alabama, from 1966–70.

Next the family lived in Harrisonburg, Virginia, where Paul earned a B.A. degree in Bible and psychology by 1972 and an M.Div. by 1976. During 1972–76 he was also Development Director for Eastern Mennonite High School and for four months interim pastor at Mt. Jackson Mennonite Church.

By 1974–75 the Mennonite Home Board was inviting him to move to Lancaster and be the Administrator. With their two youngest children, the family did move there in June 1976 (chapters above tell more of that story). In Harrisonburg, Erma worked in dietary services at the Virginia Mennonite Home; back in Lancaster County, she took a dietary job at Brethren Village near Lititz. At age 65 the couple retired and moved to Sarasota, Florida, where Paul worked half-time at Bahia Vista Mennonite Church. After three full years in Sarasota, they made Lancaster County their summer home while Paul wrote the centennial history of Mennonite Home, *On A Journey* (copies available at the Home).

They both do volunteer work, and Paul is a part-time tour guide for Mennonite Information Center, describing Amish and Mennonite beliefs and practices to tourists. They spend time with children, grandchildren, family, and friends and enjoy fellowship with the believers at Forest Hills Mennonite Church, Leola. During the summer Paul and Erma reside at 14 Conestoga Manor Village, Leola, Pa. 17540. They are pleased to share this story of their life's experiences with you as reader. God bless!

The retirees Paul and Erma Leaman on The Princess for a Galaxy Cruise in the Caribbean.